YOUR
NEW LIFE
with ADULT
CHILDREN

YOUR NEW LIFE
with ADULT
CHILDREN

A Practical Guide to What Helps, What Hurts, and What Heals

GARY CHAPMAN, PhD
& ROSS CAMPBELL, MD

MOODY PUBLISHERS
CHICAGO

This book is a revised and updated edition of *Parenting Your Adult Child* © 1999 by Ross Campbell and Gary Chapman; and *How to Really Love Your Adult Child* © 2011 by Ross Campbell and Gary Chapman.

Scriptures taken from the Holy Bible, New International Version®, NIV®. Copyright © 1973, 1978, 1984, 2011 by Biblica, Inc.™ Used by permission of Zondervan. All rights reserved worldwide. www.zondervan.com The "NIV" and "New International Version" are trademarks registered in the United States Patent and Trademark Office by Biblica, Inc.™

Edited by Pamela Joy Pugh
Interior design: Brandi Davis
Cover design: Kaylee Lockenour Dunn

Library of Congress Cataloging-in-Publication Data

Names: Chapman, Gary D., 1938- author.
Title: Your new life with adult children : a practical guide to what helps, what hurts, and what heals / Gary Chapman, PhD & Ross Campbell, MD.
Description: Chicago : Northfield Publishing, [2024] | Includes bibliographical references. | Summary: "Learn how to stay close to your adult children without infringing on their boundaries. This book will help you come to your child's aid when needed, and show your respect and unconditional love at all times. An insightful guide for the most sensitive situations"-- Provided by publisher.
Identifiers: LCCN 2023057531 (print) | LCCN 2023057532 (ebook) | ISBN 9780802434807 (paperback) | ISBN 9780802470577 (ebook)
Subjects: LCSH: Parent and adult child. | Adult children--Family relationships. | Parenting--Religious aspects.
Classification: LCC HQ755.86 .C42 2024 (print) | LCC HQ755.86 (ebook) | DDC 306.874--dc23/eng/20231227
LC record available at https://lccn.loc.gov/2023057531
LC ebook record available at https://lccn.loc.gov/2023057532

Originally delivered by fleets of horse-drawn wagons, the affordable paperbacks from D. L. Moody's publishing house resourced the church and served everyday people. Now, after more than 125 years of publishing and ministry, Moody Publishers' mission remains the same—even if our delivery systems have changed a bit. For more information on other books (and resources) created from a biblical perspective, go to www.moodypublishers.com or write to:

Moody Publishers
820 N. LaSalle Boulevard
Chicago, IL 60610

1 3 5 7 9 10 8 6 4 2

Printed in the United States of America

Contents

A Note to
the Reader

"My son seems stuck in a job with no future."

"Why don't my adult children go to church? That's not how they were raised."

"I don't like my daughter living with her partner. Why won't they just get married?"

"What's with these video games? My son is a grown man, not a child playing games."

"I hadn't expected to be raising grandchildren."

"Will they always need financial help?"

Does any of this sound familiar?

Gary Chapman and Ross Campbell teamed up nearly twenty-five years ago to write *Parenting Your Adult Child*, which was updated in 2011 as *How to Really Love Your Adult Child*. We are pleased to offer you *Your New Life with Adult Children*, the updated and revised edition of this classic.

The late Ross Campbell devoted a long career as a clinical psychiatrist to exploring the parent-child relationship and authored several bestselling books. Gary Chapman has decades of experience as a marriage and family counselor, a minister, conference speaker, radio host, and is a prolific author, well known for the 5 Love Languages series and his many other books.

one

Your Relationship with Your Adult Child

How would you describe your relationship with your adult child? Your answer to this question will reveal where you need to start or pick up if you desire a growing relationship. Because human relationships are dynamic and always changing, understanding where you are will give you some clues as to where you need to go.

Perhaps you and your adult child have a close, healthy relationship. Or perhaps relations between you have been strained. Perhaps your grown child is involved in a lifestyle that troubles you, or perhaps he is stuck and not moving ahead in life. Perhaps he has financial problems. Maybe your daughter has had a string of dysfunctional relationships and suffers from crippling low self-esteem. Perhaps her job doesn't pay enough to provide her with a living wage and she has moved back home.

How can you be the parent your child needs at this stage of his or her life? What about your own needs?

This book will cover many scenarios that affect your parenting of your adult children and offer practical ways to move forward. In most cases, you can have a positive, growing relationship with your adult children—even a friendship. Let's get started with a look at how we can be influential in their lives.

OUR ABILITY TO INFLUENCE

Too many parents minimize their own power to create a positive climate; they blame any difficulties on the child's behavior. "If Bridget would only stop dating that miserable creature, we could get along well again," one father said. Such a statement assumes that the parent is powerless until the child makes a change. This attitude of blame has led many parents to believe "there's nothing else I can do." Once they believe this myth, a fractured relationship may continue indefinitely.

Parents can't create a good relationship with a child, but they can help create a climate in which the relationship can develop.

Far more productive is this approach: "I do not like the present behavior of my adult child. I know that I can't change that behavior, but I can and will seek to have a positive influence on her."

Your attitude, words, and behavior do influence your child every time you are together. When your child drops by, look him in the eye and say sincerely, "Hi, nice to see you. You're looking good. What's going on?" You have created a climate that promotes communication. But if you merely glance up and say, "I hope you don't wear that cap at work," you have erected a major roadblock.

As parents, we must take responsibility for our own power of influence and stop blaming our children for a less than optimal relationship. We are older and should be more mature. Our children, even though grown, are on the front end of life, still trying to learn. We can go a long way in creating a good climate in which that learning can take place. Parents can't create a good relationship with a child, but they can help create a climate in which the relationship can develop.

We need to continue to evolve in our parenting roles as our children become adults. Unfortunately, many parents do not make appropriate changes so that they can reach a truly rewarding adult-to-adult relationship with their children. But when parents and adult children behave in a mature manner, all of them can experience a new meaning and joy in life.

Unfortunately, some parents look to their adult children to meet their own needs. One mother was challenged to ask herself, *Am I making my grown child an idol? Do I look to him to affirm my value as a person?* Instead, confident parents of adult children convey affection and respect to them in a healthy manner. They place genuine importance on their children's feelings and thoughts and let them know that those opinions and feelings are deeply important. They want to come to truly understand their children. They want to know how much guidance and freedom their children need. Parents who are sensitive to their children in these ways often come to the wonderful realization of how deeply they respect and value their adult children as friends.

Let's take a few moments to examine three less-than-ideal tendencies of parenting. If you believe you have been prone to any of these styles, let me encourage you that a course correction is possible.

Overprotection

Parents who insist, "Let me do it for you," fall into a trap of overprotection. They want to do for their children what, perhaps, had not been done for them during their own growing up years. However, they do so much that their children never learn to do for themselves. Their "kindness" fosters a dependency that appears in several areas of life, whether it was too much help with schoolwork, money management, or skills needed for daily living.

Some young people go into adulthood unprepared to take care of themselves. If they then marry similarly handicapped persons, they will have major conflict in marriage, as they each expect the other to be responsible.

The parent who recognizes the pattern needs to take responsibility for changing it, or their adult child will be dependent for a lifetime.

Overprotective parents usually accept one or two false beliefs. The first is that a child cannot make it without the parent's constant involvement. The second is that the parent cannot bear the thought of a child—even an adult child—having any pain or problems out in the real world. Ironically, this is most prevalent in parents who have had to survive great hardships and have emerged as competent people. Instead of realizing that their hardships are what made them strong and competent, they desire that their children have problem-free lives with no character-building trials. They forget that it takes preparation and training to be able to function and prosper in a world that is far from being user-friendly. Part of this training is to experience difficulty, for there is no other way to learn to deal with the normal stresses of life.

This parenting style is very difficult to change, but the parent who recognizes the pattern needs to take responsibility for changing it, or their adult child will be dependent for a lifetime. The older the child, the more difficult to break the pattern. But failure to break the pattern will eventually result in greater pain for both.

Steve and Lynda's Story

Still, the pattern can be broken later, as one couple would tell you. Steve and Lynda realized their dependency patterns with Monica only when their daughter had graduated from college. Prior to that, they had paid all of Monica's college living expenses, including giving her a credit card and paying her bills. Every two or three weeks, she would come home from school for the weekend, bringing her dirty clothes to be washed and enjoying home cooking without offering to help.

The way Steve and Lynda saw it, they were just glad that Monica came home often; they felt thankful that they could take care of her expenses. They thought Monica respected them and felt as close to them as they did to her.

These feelings began to change, however, when Monica moved in with a girlfriend after graduation. Her parents thought she was on her way to establishing her own lifestyle but wondered why she continued to bring home her laundry. One day they got a call from her roommate saying that Monica had not paid her part of the rent for the past two months and had also borrowed money that she hadn't repaid. "I know you two are close to Monica," she said, "and I just thought that before this gets out of hand perhaps you could talk to her about it."

Steve and Lynda were shocked. As they talked through the situation with each other, they realized that their parenting style had not taught Monica to manage money or take responsibility. They knew that if they did not do something to help their daughter change her habits, and quickly, she could be in serious trouble.

Meanwhile, Monica was struggling with the pressures of her new job. She knew that she was not doing well in handling her money, and she didn't respond well when her parents confronted her with what they had learned. Through angry tears she said, "I feel like you're disappointed with me and don't trust me with money. I thought you wanted to do my laundry and to have me come for meals."

"We do want you to come over for meals," her father said. "We enjoy being with you, but we also want you to learn how to cook and do your own laundry. We realize that we have failed to teach you both of these things. About the money, it's not that we don't trust you but that we now know we haven't given you any help in understanding how to manage money. We feel that this is an area of parenting where we have failed you."

After a few more rounds of words and tears trying to understand one another, they all agreed that some changes would be in order, for Monica's own good. However, she had been dependent on her parents for so long that her behavior patterns were not going to change quickly. In the early stages of their plan, Steve and Lynda rescued her a few times from financial situations, until they realized that this was not helping her. They had to allow her car to be repossessed when she failed to meet the monthly payments. This was very difficult for them, but they knew they could not rescue her again. In the beginning, Monica accused them of abandoning her.

Over the next months, Monica did learn how to handle her money, how to do her laundry, fix meals, and numerous other tasks that her parents had done for her. Eventually, she got another car, and took care of routine maintenance.

In her late twenties, Monica married a fine man she met at work. He was glad he had married someone who knew how to get things done and told his in-laws he hoped that when the time came, he would raise his children as well as they had raised Monica. They smiled at each other and thanked their new son-in-law. That night at home, they congratulated each other on the hard work they had done over the last several years in helping Monica become independent.

> A comic strip character was bemoaning the challenges of raising parents. "Nothing I try to teach her sinks in," he said, exasperated. "You never know how tough life can be until you have parents of your own."[1]

Undermanagement

Parents who do not give enough management to their children's lives can be of various types. Some may seem distant and unapproachable, and not know how to care for their child's emotional needs. Many undermanage because they fear displeasing their children, even losing their love; some give minimal input because they dislike conflict. Others may be overly permissive; still others have devoted little time to their children's lives because of their own busy or long work schedules, which often leave them tired when they arrive home.

Those parents who seem distant usually grew up in homes where their own parents provided for physical needs but failed to relate to them on an emotional level. Consequently, they have only vague ideas of how to develop such a relationship with their own children. These parents need to work toward understanding the

For parents who realize that they have a distant relationship with their adult children, a change in lifestyle is called for.

value of emotional closeness with their children. Ideally, this would be done when the children are young, but it is never too late to learn.

For parents who realize that they have a distant relationship with their adult children, a change in lifestyle is called for. You can no longer do what you have always done if you want to minimize the weakness of this parenting style. If your problem is that you are too busy working or helping others or just uncomfortable being open and transparent, you need to pay attention and begin connecting with your children, even those who are grown and out of your home.

Mark was one such parent. Mark is the father of two sons. When they were both in their twenties and still single, he started to notice that, while cordial at family get-togethers, his sons didn't seem to have much to say to him but were more conversant with their mother. It dawned on Mark that he had done little to develop a relationship with the boys as they were growing up, and he wondered if it was too late to change that.

Mark first talked with his wife about this and then with his sons, sharing with them his sense of having let them down. He told them: "To the best of my ability, I want to change this starting now. I know I spent many hours at work during your childhood, maybe more than I should have, but I did that with you in mind. However, that's no excuse for not spending more time with you."

Josh and his older brother Brad were somewhat uncomfortable with Mark's confession, but they both agreed to try to be intentional in spending more time together. They began meeting for breakfast every other Saturday and attended sporting events together. As the weeks and months went on, both young men began to be more open with Mark about their interests and even uncertainties. Mark had rarely talked with his own father about personal matters, so his parenting style naturally flowed to a hands-off approach.

But as time went on since Mark confessed to his sons that he had been uninvolved, both sons have developed a much closer relationship with their dad. Brad sought his advice before buying a car and Josh asked—and listened to—his opinion on whether to return to college or try a trade school. He mentioned certifying in heating and cooling, with the draw of being able to start a good job without student loan debt. When Brad took a job in a distant suburb, the in-person meetings were not as frequent, but Mark purposed to text or phone him at least once a week. Mark just wishes that his eyes had been opened earlier to the value of giving more time and attention to his children.

———

Why have some parents gotten into the habit of undermanaging their children? Some parents who undermanage their children simply hate conflict. When the children realize this at whatever age, they are eager to take advantage of it. Even if we have an aversion to conflict, we must remind ourselves that our children need to learn good values and skills, many of which they may not encounter unless we provide the kind of direction we should.

Those parents who are very permissive choose to be uninvolved, even subconsciously. Their thinking is that their children can do as they please—even in situations where direction, protection, or control is needed. These parents need to be more aware of what is appropriate freedom or responsibility for various age levels. Also, they need to be more cautious in a dangerous world.

Most parents who undermanage their children do so because they have been confused about parenting and were afraid of displeasing their children, even losing their love. They either struggled with their own self-esteem, or they misunderstand the true meaning of discipline during the childrearing years.[2]

Micromanagement

With this parenting style, the parents are deeply involved with their children, devoting much energy to help their offspring learn and grow. Since the children's earliest years, the parents sought to give their children auditory and visual stimuli to develop their intellectual capacities. They gave lots of hugs and kisses and affirming words to meet the children's emotional needs. They attended every ball game, musical recital, and spelling bee.

The description sounds positive, doesn't it? Now, as their children move into adulthood, they intend to continue being good parents. The problem is that they fail to shift gears, and the young adults who are seeking independence feel dominated. Thus, they draw away from their parents, spending less time with them and asking for advice less frequently. This hurts the parents, who feel that their children are abandoning them.

The solution? Parents whose style is intense, hands-on management need to draw back, pray more and probe less, and give their children the freedom to make decisions on their own.

Micromanaging a child can also mean handling the child with an authoritarian attitude, being a boss to the child; even, in a sense, playing God. It can mean giving orders as though the child were a Marine recruit. This is fine in the military, but no way to "start children off on the way they should go."[3] This approach may seem to work when the child is small, but it is actually counterproductive. It does not teach a child to interact with you or others in healthy and meaningful ways. Therefore, you are depriving your child of the privilege of learning the skills of social interaction. She cannot learn to carry on pleasant small talk, an increasingly critical skill as more and more communication between people is done in brief spurts by texting, complete with emojis and GIFs, or on other social media. She will be hampered in learning to make decisions and think for herself. A child who is continually told what to do and how to think will struggle with learning how to manage life.

An adult child who was—or is still being—micromanaged probably displays anti-authority behavior toward employers.

Micromanagement leaves the child no other emotional recourse than to become angry. Since there is little room for discussion or the teaching of verbal skills to handle the anger, the child's anger will emerge in unhealthy ways. An adult child who was—or is still being—micromanaged probably displays anti-authority behavior toward employers and others. Many religious parents use the micromanagement approach to parenting, partly because they have been taught that this is what God desires. However, such an approach will backfire on them when the children reach adulthood. Maybe you've already noticed this with your adult children.

Besides developing anger, the child reared by the overmanaging parental style will likely fail to learn to accept responsibility for his own behavior. All around us we see people who have never learned this, so they see themselves as perpetual victims. Everything is someone else's fault.

The negatives of this parenting style need not continue. Vince and Teresa had both had meddlesome parents who micromanaged. When the couple married, they struggled to free themselves from the interference of two sets of parents. Teresa's mother called her every day, asking what she was doing at the moment, reminding her to wear a warm hat on cold days, offering to drop by with a nutritious meal—and often did without asking first. Her father was always at Vince with "better" ideas about car maintenance and home repairs, often undoing something Vince had already completed.

When the couple was on vacation and Teresa's parents had a key so they could bring in the mail and "check that everything's okay," they painted the kitchen "a more durable color." Vince and Teresa decided they'd had enough. Though it was awkward, they sat the parents down and explained how much they valued their relationship and interest in their lives. Then they plunged in with the changes they expected to begin immediately. They repeated the discussion with Vince's parents.

Parents who seek to teach their children to make decisions by allowing them the freedom to do so will likely minimize the tendency to meddle in the lives of their young adults. They will be there for their children, but they will not dominate. One wise boundary many parents have set for themselves is not to give their married children advice unless requested. Sharing this self-imposed boundary with children before they marry is a good way to let them hold you accountable for staying within the boundary you yourself have set.

YOU CAN DO IT

It is crucial to understand that no one has done a perfect job with their children. Parenting is about the most difficult job in the world, and few of us have had any training in it. Yet, even if you had the best training in the world, there are still situations that no one can foresee, and some that almost no one can cope with well. Every family is different and every child unique. When we admit that we have made mistakes, and when we understand just how and when we misjudged, we can begin to do something about it.

> "At life's banquet of success I may not be the guest of honor, but I'll be among those present."
> — Emily in *Emily Climbs* by Lucy Maud Montgomery

Most parents have done something right. It is helpful to make a list of all the ways you have been a good parent. You should enumerate them, from the small acts to the most sacrificial, to help you see the whole picture. You want to focus on the complete relationship with your child, not only on what has gone wrong. Emphasize the positive aspects of your bond with your child and what you have done well.

A PARENT'S POSITIVE LOVE

Adult children are most open to the influence of those who love them. This is often why they are so receptive to the influence of peers and closed to their parents. Their friends give them acceptance and affirmation, and their parents may give them condemnation. Parents who wish to be a positive influence must focus on meeting their children's need for emotional love. But how can we parents make our children feel they are loved?

We do this by assuring our adult children in many ways that "I love you, no matter what." At times, we may not like their behavior, but that doesn't mean we withhold our love. To do so is to love them "only if . . ." which is not true love. It is okay to tell your child, "I may not like what you are doing, but it will not keep me from loving you." This is true unconditional parental love.

SPEAK THE LOVE LANGUAGES[4]

As you seek to meet your son's or daughter's need for emotional love, it is important to realize that not everyone understands the same love language. What makes one person feel loved will not necessarily make another feel that way. Thus, your child may not sense your love if you are speaking or expressing your love in a way (language) she doesn't understand. In my years as a pastor and counselor, I found patterns indicating that there are five basic languages of love and that each person will understand one of them more deeply than the other four. It is the parents' job to know the primary love language of their adult child and to give heavy doses of love in this language.

Here is a brief description of the five languages. Each of these languages represents a different way you can express love. Again, your adult child will most sense your love when you speak her language (although our children need to receive expressions of love in all five languages).

1. Words of Affirmation. You use words to build up or affirm the person. "You look nice today . . . Thanks for feeding the dog . . . I appreciate your bringing in the mail while I was gone . . . Your car looks great . . . I like your apartment." To the person whose love language is *words of affirmation*, all these statements express love. "Your boss must have really been pleased. This report is impressive . . . I'm proud that you are my son/daughter . . . You are a wonderful parent to your babies." Such statements are appropriate words of affirmation for young adults.

2. Gifts. The bestowing of gifts is a universal language of love. A gift says, "He was thinking of me. Look at what he brought me." Phil knew that his twentysomething son Darren had collected Coke bottles when he was in junior high and still had the bottles stored in his apartment. During a business trip to Egypt, Phil bought Darren a Coke bottle with Arabic writing. When he gave it to him on his return, Phil saw the biggest smile he had seen in years. The reason was that, to Darren, the gift said to him: "Dad remembered. He cares." Gifts need not be expensive; they may be as simple as a stone picked up on a hiking trail—or a Coke bottle. They are visual symbols that someone cares.

3. Acts of Service. This involves doing things that you know will be appreciated. Cooking a favorite meal or dessert, repairing a mechanical device, keeping your son's pet or children while he and your daughter-in-law are on vacation, mowing their grass when he isn't feeling well—all of these are more than acts of kindness. They are speaking love on an emotional level, for they demonstrate that you care. And if this is your adult child's primary love language, such acts make your son or daughter feel loved.

4. Quality Time. In spending quality time with your child, you are giving her your undivided attention, really giving a part of your life, so that she has all of you at that moment. Quality time may include taking a walk together or crafting or going to a movie together. The important thing is not the activity but being together. Conversations are part of most expressions of quality time. Conversations are enhanced by eye contact. Wise parents give focused attention when their young adult starts talking. Being an intentional listener speaks volumes.

5. Physical Touch. The language of physical touch may include a hug when the child comes for a visit, a pat on the back as he enters the room, sitting close enough to touch shoulders as you watch TV or a movie together, a hand on the shoulder as you serve him a soda. All of these express love through touch.

Requests and Suggestions

Our love tank is the part of us that represents our need for emotional love. If you are expressing love to your child and thereby keeping his or her love tank full, you probably know that *requests are more productive than demands.* No one likes to be controlled, and demands are efforts at controlling. Demands may get results, but they are almost always accompanied by resentment.

I'm not suggesting that you should never resort to demanding anything of your young adult children, especially those who still live in your home. Just keep them as a last effort, not the first. Requests should always be as specific as possible, since general requests are ambiguous and seldom get the desired results.

I also recommend that you *give suggestions rather than proclamations*, especially when your child is grown and out of the house. "You need to get this application in today or you are not going to get the job" is a proclamation. It assumes that you know everything. "You know what I would suggest? That you try to finish up that application and submit it. Probably the sooner you do that, the more likely you are to get an interview and perhaps the job" is a suggestion. Young adults tend to respond much more positively to suggestions than they do proclamations.

When we come across as issuing decrees, our adult children are likely to dismiss them and not give them serious thought. However, when we offer suggestions, we are acknowledging our humanity and limited experience. We are simply sharing our best thoughts, which they are more likely to receive as such, and give them due consideration.

HOPE FROM THE BIBLE

Some of us have forgotten how to be confident in a fallen world. Parenting has changed just as our world has changed. Our children have grown, and we keep having to learn the next lessons.

By this time, we are well aware of the mistakes we have made and that we are far from perfect parents. And yet, we ourselves can go on to greater maturity and be ready to make the necessary changes for the future. And we can help our children move to maturity as well.

You can find inspiration, comfort, and confidence in parenting in the Bible. I encourage you to read the many words of wisdom and encouragement it gives concerning our children, even those who are grown. Two that come to mind are "Children are a heritage from the LORD, offspring a reward from him" and "From everlasting to everlasting the LORD's love is with those who fear [respect] him, and his righteousness with their children's children."[5]

Other verses of hope include Psalm 112:2; Isaiah 44:3–5; 54:13; and Jeremiah 31:17. Such verses can sustain parents who are concerned and prayerful about their children.

Obstacles on the Path to Independence

two

___

When Your Adult Child Is Stuck

When Barbara came across the comic strip "Dustin"—about an unmotivated college grad who moved back in with his parents—she immediately related to that young man's mother.

Barbara's twenty-two-year-old son finished college in May and spent the summer enjoying himself. It is now October and Tyson is not looking for work. He spends his evenings hanging out with friends, arrives home after midnight, and sleeps half the morning. He spends far too much time online. Some days he is still at home when Barbara returns from her office. When he is, they talk for a while and then he is off to see his friends.

Barbara was willing to accept his inactivity for the summer, thinking that perhaps he needed a break after his college years. But now that summer is long gone, she is very concerned. She often wonders what he is going to do; but when she asks Tyson about this, he answers, "I don't know what I want to do." Once he talked about his friend Brian, who was teaching English as a second language in

Budapest. He thought he might go and "hang out" with Brian for a while.

"Where will you get the money for that?" Barbara asked.

"I'll work. That won't be a problem."

Barbara had hope. But Tyson hasn't mentioned Brian lately.

Barbara doesn't understand why Tyson won't try to find a job so he can save money, get his own place, and begin to get on with adulthood. Anytime she talks to Tyson about her expectation that he will move toward being independent, his response is unsettling.

"Why? Why would I want to tie myself down to a regular job at this point in my life?" he typically answers. "Maybe someday, if I ever have a family, but not now. This is the time to hang loose, experience life, read, think, and meditate."

Barbara and her husband had split up many years ago and Tyson doesn't often see his dad. When they do get together, they end up arguing about Tyson's future, especially since his father helped pay for college. For now, Tyson finds it easier to stay away from his dad. He knows his mother has the same questions, but at least she isn't argumentative.

THE RIGHT APPROACH

Tyson's parents represent millions of parents who just can't understand what is going on. They have loved their children and have done what they could for them within the imperfect circumstances of their own lives. And now that those children are grown, they are not living in ways that their parents consider to be mature.

If you find yourself in such a situation, you are having to deal not only with your child but also with yourself. If you take time to look inside, you will find some conflicting emotions that affect your relationship with your child. All parents have these mixed feelings to an extent, but for you just now they are heightened by the behavior of your child. In addition to the love and hopefulness you feel for your son or daughter, you also are experiencing some level of guilt and anxiety about your own role as a parent. You may be asking yourself, "Is it my fault? What should I have done differently?" You may even be thinking of some specific incidents and wondering if they were the catalysts that derailed your child.

Because these feelings of guilt and anxiety can complicate your relationship with your adult child, it is very important that you come to understand yourself and your emotions. Unless you deal with your anxiety and guilt, they will cause you more pain and confusion than you already have. And they may motivate you to take actions that you will later regret.

> "It is important to understand what it is that you are feeling guilty about and why you feel this way. Try to make sure you are keeping the expectations you place on yourself in perspective and realistic. Try to remember that the reason you feel guilty is because you care—which is the most important thing. Striking the balance of caring while also being realistic and keeping perspective is a fine art. It may take some time and discipline, but it is a key to managing parent guilt."[1]

This combination of guilt and anxiety can cause you to react inappropriately toward your adult child typically in one of two ways.

Hands-Off

The first kind of inappropriate response is to become permissive. This happens when parents feel so guilty about past mistakes that they allow the adult child to manipulate them and to give in to unreasonable demands. Fred and Lissie have one son, Tom. When he graduated from college, he took a job near the school, but he didn't enjoy it and quit after six months. He returned home and has been living with his parents. Tom is not hostile to his parents and seems to like spending time with them. When they go out to eat, Fred, of course, picks up everyone's tab. And when Tom asks for money, Fred can't say no.

Both guilt and fear control Fred. He thinks that he was not a good father to Tom, and he fears that Tom will somehow reject him or will become depressed and discouraged if he doesn't give him what he wants. Lissie strongly disagrees with Fred on this; she thinks Tom is quite capable of taking care of himself. She tries to convince Fred that he has been a good father and that he shouldn't let his guilt feelings control his relationship with Tom. She also believes that giving in to Tom is not helping his self-esteem. In fact, the more dependent he is, the worse he will feel about himself. Lissie finally persuades Fred to pursue family counseling so that they can learn to deal with their son in a more helpful and healthy manner.

Anger

A second way that guilt and anxiety can influence parental behaviors involves yet another emotion: anger. Fear and anxiety can cause feelings of anger. Guilt can easily spur anger until it controls the parents' reactions of disappointment toward their adult child. Improper management of this anger can be harmful and even permanently destructive to the parent-child relationship.

John and Pam are parents to twenty-four-year-old Sandi, whose behavior is similar to Tom's. The difference in these families is that John becomes so distressed with Sandi's irresponsibility that he occasionally loses his temper and shouts at her, criticizing her inability to "get herself together." Of course, this hurts Sandi and breaks communication between them, often for days at a time. As John continues to vent his anger on Sandi, their relationship is slowly dying. Pam suffers immeasurably as she sees the growing distance between her two precious loved ones. This family also needs to seek outside help before the alienation gets to the point of no return.

It's crucial that we show self-control in our relationships with our adult children. This will enable our children to more easily communicate with us and will also provide a model of mature behavior. The better you do during this difficult time, the better your child will do. Your most important job just now is to maintain and attempt to improve your relationship with your grown child. Only in this way can you teach him to respect and love himself.

EVERY SITUATION CAN BE IMPROVED

Show Love

All of us suffer feelings of low self-esteem at times, but for young adults, these feelings can be very intense. In part, they reflect a society that cares less and less about the individual and, as parents, you are in the best position to help. You have the opportunity to influence your child for a lifetime; your love and emotional nurture can help your child move toward the maturity you long to see.

Simply loving your child during these agonizing periods is not taking a hands-off approach; you are not condoning her mistakes or failures. Loving your adult child unconditionally and unfailingly will help her resume her growth toward mature thinking and behavior. If you react unlovingly and unpleasantly, you are complicating everyone's life.

Be Optimistic

While your child has had to face enormous change, you may feel you have had to face the unexpected: an adult child who is immature and unproductive. You may wonder, *How? How can I help someone who acts like he hasn't grown up?* As a family counselor, I have seen many situations in which young adults fell into disappointing behavior. In most of these, when the parents were loving toward them, the adult children were able to resume growth toward maturity and overcome their difficulties. Parents with children in trouble or slow to mature must remember that each such situation can be helped.

There is reason to be optimistic. Although adult children may seem to react negatively to every effort, they will eventually absorb their parents' love, hope, and optimism. They can change. Parents going through this kind of ordeal need to believe that God cares, and that He is especially sensitive to the feelings of hurting parents.[2]

Understand Your Son's or Daughter's Point of View

A bridge that many parents are unable to cross is being so bound by their own outlook on life and what they believe to be best for their children that they find it almost impossible to see the world through the eyes of these young adults.

For example, Barbara sees the world through a traditional mindset, as she had been brought up. Tyson sees the world in a vastly different manner. His generation has been influenced to believe that there are no cultural or moral absolutes. To be rich is no more desirable than to be poor. To be married certainly does not bring more happiness than being single. Tyson does want to be connected; that is why hanging with his friends is so important. But he doesn't want the responsibility of being tied down to one person, at least not yet, nor does he want to be in a job that he fears might become drudgery.

The age-old question "What is the purpose of life?" still rumbles in the minds of Tyson and his peers, but they are not sure there is an answer. That is why life for Tyson and so many others is simply surfing, drifting, looking, thinking, and sometimes even hoping that they will make a significant discovery that will give life ultimate meaning.

If we parents are to serve as their mentors, we must remove any barriers that have been built up over time and then learn to communicate.

If their parents are to play a positive role in their lives, they must first of all understand their children's viewpoint about the world and their place in it. Some of the tension is generational. That is, Barbara grew up in a different era with different expectations than Tyson and his contemporaries.

So at this juncture, how is Barbara going to relate to Tyson in a constructive manner and not fall into the argumentative pattern that has developed between her son and his father? Let's consider how she can deal with the tension that threatens to alienate her son and her. Doing so suggests several ways we can deal with our own children and help them to maturity and success.

Be Vulnerable and Real

Barbara should be willing to be vulnerable, open, and real. When she does that—when any parent does that—she receives the child's respect and often the right to be a mentor. Barbara already feels that she has been vulnerable, but this is going to call for an even larger dose. She and anyone with children in this stage need to admit our own frustrations and disappointments with life and acknowledge that we ourselves have made some poor decisions. Being honest about our own struggles with life's meaning is a prerequisite to effectively giving any insights we believe will help our children in their search for satisfaction.

It is not that young adults are not looking for guidance. They do want advice, encouragement, and support, but from people they respect. If we parents are to serve as their mentors, we must remove any barriers that have been built up over time and then learn to communicate—not as all-knowing parents but as individuals still in the lifelong process of learning. We need to share our thoughts as ideas rather than dogma. When our children see us as helpers rather than controllers, they are more likely to be influenced by our ideas. Our children can and will dialogue with us if we are willing to create a nonthreatening and nonjudgmental atmosphere.

Recognize That Your Vision Differs from Your Child's

Barbara needs to accept the reality that her visions of what Tyson ought to do are not his visions. She needs to respect him as an individual and give him the freedom to think, dream, and view life differently than she does. According to the Judeo-Christian worldview, this is what God does with us. He gives us the freedom to think our own thoughts and make our own decisions, even when they are not in keeping with His. This does not mean that our thoughts are as valid as God's, but it does mean that God values human freedom and does not wish to treat us as robots.

Parents who want to relate to their young adult children in an authentic way should remember that truth: each person has distinct thoughts and the right to make decisions in his or her way.

Our children's vision of the future and their choices in the future are theirs to make, and we must respect those choices, even if our children will suffer the consequences of wrong decisions.

Begin an Honest Dialogue

Barbara can begin an honest dialogue with her son. By giving Tyson the freedom to dream and choose, Barbara has opened the door for dialogue. She can now discuss with him the implications of choices within that framework and talk about where certain courses of action may lead. She may share examples from her own experience, since she is not using them as a club but as a flashlight to identify the realities in the path ahead.

For instance, she could now discuss with Tyson the question, "Do you think I am helping you or hurting you by allowing you to live here with me without paying any rent or contributing to other expenses? I am not asking this to manipulate you but in an honest effort to help both of us think about what is best for you." Such a question and the ensuing discussion may well lead to a meaningful look at the importance and value of daily necessities and what one must do to acquire them. This is especially important for an adult child like Tyson who, by putting off finding work, thought that he was above the mundane details of life. In such a conversation, Tyson may realize that his lack of work, far from enhancing his own self-worth, is in effect destroying it.

Barbara might want to move to something like this: "What do you think Brian is getting out of teaching English in Budapest?" Tyson might answer that his friend finds satisfaction in helping others. They are now discussing the idea that one road to finding one's significance is through service. It may well be the motivation Tyson needs to add another dimension to his life.

Such a dialogue is usually effective. It communicates respect for your son's opinion, helps you understand him better, and can help him sort through options. Pursuing a dialogue whenever possible is the recommended course; it is always preferable to a one-sided lecture.

Another Approach

What if Tyson is still not motivated to find work? Barbara may need to consider taking a hard line. If she is convinced that her financial support of her son is to his own detriment, and if she has seen no movement toward getting a job, she may well say, "So Tyson, I've been thinking about our conversation some weeks ago. I've come to believe that I'm doing you a great disservice to let you continue to live here with me without making any financial contribution. I think this is fostering your dependence on me and is hindering you from developing an independent lifestyle. Therefore, starting next month, if you want to continue to live here, I'll expect you to pay for housing and contribute to grocery and utility expenses. Of course, if you want to make other arrangements, I'll understand. I just believe it is my responsibility to do what I can to help you develop an independent lifestyle."

At times this uncompromising approach can accomplish what a more tender plan of action has not. Both techniques are born of love. Though the child may suffer (for a season) from your withholding aid and permitting adverse consequences to come, the purpose is loving: his maturing by learning and acting independently. Keep in mind, though, that the hard line is used only after other more congenial approaches have failed. It is not the place to begin.

OTHER ISSUES TO ADDRESS
IF YOUR ADULT CHILD IS STUCK

Not all young adults who seem uninterested in launching into responsible living are like Tyson. Many of them have been raised in healthy—often religious—homes, and they hold to traditional values such as working to provide a living. Yet they too can and at times do struggle with the move to adulthood. Their apparent lack of or limited success is due to various causes. These adult children may have done poorly in school, work, or family and social relationships. The parents may bemoan their seeming immaturity.

When you discover the cause(s) of the poor performance, you can help your children take appropriate steps. Three reasons an adult may struggle are a rebellious spirit, low self-esteem, and emotional and relational barriers.

A Rebellious Spirit

Some young adults fail to achieve because they are angry with their parents and are subconsciously trying to hurt them. Psychologists commonly call this passive-aggressive behavior, which we'll flesh out more in chapter 5. Because they seem passive on the outside, their parents don't often observe the anger or rage that lies beneath. But the person's behavior is showing that it is there.

By his action or lack of action, the rebelling young adult is saying, "You will not control my life. You will not tell me what is important in my life." The harder the parent presses this child to be successful, whether in school or in other areas of life, the more the child will resist.

Low Self-Esteem

Low self-esteem is a common emotional malady, affecting many young adults. Our culture has exalted the beautiful, the intelligent, the athletic, the talented. Yet, most of our population does not fall into these categories. Consequently, thousands of young people are plagued by feelings of inferiority and even worthlessness when they compare themselves to their peers or siblings. These inner feelings of insecurity often keep them from reaching their potential in school, at work, or in human relationships.

You can detect if this is the case for your child by listening to what he says. Such statements as "I'm not sure I can do it," "I'm not as good as Trent," "I'm afraid to try," "I'm not cut out to be a manager," or "I just can't get it," are telling you that the problem may be low self-esteem.

> Success is not final, failure is not fatal: it is the courage to continue that counts.
> —Winston Churchill

Other young people perform poorly at work because they do not have sufficient background academically or emotionally to handle the requirements, or because—accurately or not—they believe they are in a pattern of poor results they cannot break. When this happens in the workplace, especially in environments of fast-paced changed, the young person may believe he or she will invariably fall short and not believe they have a shot at success. These young adults may be passed over for promotions and eventually even lose their jobs if this inadequacy is not taken care of.

Emotional and Relational Barriers

Accompanying low self-esteem, other disabling emotional problems—including anxiety, depression, poor motivation, and problems in relating to others—may cling to adult children entering the workplace. One irony in our world is that "we're more connected but lonelier than ever." According to a report from the US Surgeon General, we are in a loneliness epidemic. Though loneliness in itself is not something new, the rise and proliferation of social media has intensified disconnection. Licensed clinical therapist Jenn Oxborrow puts it this way: "Digital social messaging and social connection should be one of the many ways we connect." But, she warns, "when it replaces all of the ways that we connect, we start to see that isolation."[3] Parents of adult children need to understand the significance of this observation.

Many people today need help in these emotional and relational areas. Some need help overcoming patterns of behavior, attitude, or repeated disappointment. Some need good mental health services in order to adequately function in society, and a mentoring parent can research and help seek out these for their adult child.

TO WRAP UP

Unless you discover the reason for poor performance and reasons your adult child is stuck, you will not be able to help. The primary means of discovering what is going on in your child's life is to communicate, to have conversation as a peer rather than as a parent. Taking a judgmental attitude, complete with verbal tirades, simply puts more distance between the two of you. It is far more productive to ask sensitive questions designed to help you understand what she is thinking and feeling. Then wait for her to ask those simple words "What do you think?" before making suggestions.

When we feel they need prodding to get somewhere, we need to look for areas that deserve commendation.

Unsolicited advice will almost always produce a negative response. But when your grown child feels that you genuinely care and understand, she is far more likely to receive your counsel.

Just like everyone else, young adults welcome words of encouragement. When we are troubled by their poor performance and feel they need prodding to get somewhere, we need to look for areas that deserve commendation. Our tendency too often is to say nothing about their small successes because we feel their potential is so much greater. But affirming their minor accomplishments tends to motivate a more positive response. In contrast, condemning words tend to generate negative feelings.

If you conclude that your adult child has low self-esteem, encouraging words will be especially helpful. "You've done a nice job fixing up your room. It really looks nice" is certainly to be preferred to "Why are you still painting your room? You should be looking for a job." Similarly, "That's a good sound—I like the rhythm" is better than "Why are you on the drums? Nothing better to do?" Young adults tend to perform best in areas in which they have a personal interest.

If your child is not living in your home, you may have to be more intentional about finding ways to affirm with words. "What do you think about this car I'm thinking of buying? I value your opinion." "You're so kind to the server. I like going to lunch with you. A lot of people would be critical and complain." "Can you suggest a gift for your sister's birthday? You always have good ideas."

When we commend our children's successes in key areas, even though those areas may not be important to us, we create motivation to succeed in other areas. When we belittle or condemn their efforts because we think they should be spending their time and energy somewhere else, we create a negative climate and emotional distance between us. The ancient Hebrew proverb is true: "The tongue has the power of life and death."[4] Affirm your grown children, and they may feel renewed zeal to try again and succeed.

three

When the Nest Isn't Emptying

An old TV commercial featured parents feigning sadness as they waved to their daughter leaving home for college. As the young woman drove away, one parent wistfully said, "There she goes. Off to the big city." In the next scene, the newly empty nesters were seen living it up on a carefree vacation, whirling on rides at the amusement park, dining and dancing at an upscale restaurant. It was an entertaining ad, but how realistic is this scenario?

We might expect our children to leave the home nest shortly after finishing high school. But that isn't universally the case today. For a variety of reasons, many of our children who are in their late teens and early twenties—or older—are still in the family home. In this chapter, we'll explore parenting your young adult who fits this situation, focusing especially on the older teen or younger twenty-something. In the next chapter, we'll talk more about adult children who move back home.

JUMBLED EMOTIONS

Though the parenting years are generally a mix of busy, challenging, and joyful, parents in general are ready for the next season, when the children are no longer in the family home. They look forward to having more time for themselves and for each other, and to developing a daily routine that no longer revolves around their offspring.

However, there is still an adjustment for the new season of the parents' life. Whether children have left one by one, or whether an only child is grown up and suddenly the home atmosphere is different, this is still a time of transition for parents too. This is especially true for a mother who has dedicated herself to child-rearing. She now may be more free to seek employment outside the home, take classes, or spend more time volunteering. But she might also have a period of feeling adrift. She may feel—and we're not omitting dads here—like she's on an "emotional roller coaster of this new, disorienting season of life."[1] These parents aren't necessarily eager to have their children out of the home altogether. Both adult children and parents can be validated that their "roller coaster" of emotions during this time are normal and healthy.

WHEN THE NEST FEELS WARM

Eventually though, both grown children and their parents adjust to the new reality. However, the flight out of the family nest is often bumpier and takes longer than expected, and many parents find that the nest is still occupied. The reasons for older teens and early twenty-somethings staying with parents often make sense, though they don't lighten the parents' duties. One major factor is economics.

But even beyond financial factors, in a society where people are connected by social media yet still lonely (as mentioned in chapter 2), and in a time of fewer shared values and greater ideological conflict, many young people feel anxious and pessimistic. They want to extend the transition to adulthood and independence.

For other young adults the cost of higher education keeps them homebound. Today more students are attending local colleges and continuing to live with their parents. Or, they may go to their state university but return often for home cooking, to do their laundry for free, or just to hang around. Yet once they are in college, they expect to be treated differently at home, wishing to come and go as they please. They have people to see and things to do, and they don't plan to spend a weekend at home visiting with their parents.

> In a Harris Poll, "a large majority of respondents reported they were sympathetic toward those who choose to live with their families, with 87% saying they think people shouldn't be judged for living at home."[2]

THE NESTING SYNDROME

The Plus Side of the Coin

For both parents and their adult children living in the home, the extended time together can be a very positive experience. It provides young adults a needed and limited period of time to prepare themselves for independence. This is especially important if they value the quality of their family life and find strength and encouragement there. Home becomes a place of shelter for those not yet able to deal with the anxieties they find in an uncertain world, as well as a place where grown children can start to get on their feet financially. For parents who find it hard to part with their children all at once—one described the feeling "like a forced retirement with no celebration"[3]—the additional time their children live at home provides them a valuable transition.

The Other Side of the Coin

Yet it is true that many parents have questions about the nesting syndrome, especially about their roles and attitudes. Even those who find the experience of having their grown children at home generally positive wonder at times if they are being too permissive and soft with their children. They don't know what limits and rules are appropriate. Also, they don't always know how to handle the changing expectations of their children in relation to them. Other parents are uneasy about having their children stay at home, while some are openly angry at what they regard as an imposition.

Almost everyone can make a continuing nesting experience a growing and exciting adventure for the entire family. Not that it will be easy . . .

If you are a not-quite-empty-nester, you know that you are dealing with a complicated mix of expectations and emotions that are not going to go away or resolve themselves. You may also be perplexed about the best way to handle your situation. Regardless of the varying expectations of parents and young adult children, almost everyone can make a continuing nesting experience a growing and exciting adventure for the entire family. Not that it will be easy, but, as in all relationships, a little work will pay off in huge dividends.

Even if your adult child remains at home, keep in mind that you are still parenting, although in somewhat different ways. As in all parenting situations, you want to do all you can to give your child your love and care and direction, regardless of the stress you or your child may be feeling. It is also important that you stay clear of two parental traps: coming down too hard and being too easygoing, as was mentioned in the first chapter. If you can do this, while at the same time refusing to give in to negative feelings, your child will come sooner to maturity and independence. Make your home atmosphere as warm, upbeat, and supportive as possible, a place for making positive memories for everyone.

Families who have lived through the unempty nest period may feel tensions but also reap rewards. Let's look at two families who have grown through the adult children's presence in the home.

Neal and Brenna's Story

Neal and Brenna Collier have two children. Their son, Adam, is twenty-three and taking courses to certify as a phlebotomist. He lives with his parents. Adam tried one year at the state university but dropped out during his second semester because he was doing poorly. His failure was due to two factors: lack of good study habits and a propensity to party rather than study. He came home, regrouped, took a summer school course in study skills, found a part-time job with a car rental company, landed on a career interest, and now is doing fairly well with his training.

His sister, Jessi, is twenty-one and a sophomore at the state university, planning on earning a four-year nursing degree. She comes home every few weekends; sometimes she brings a friend but usually comes alone.

Jessi always lets her parents know a few days before she'll arrive. Neal, the weekend cook for the family, prepares one of Jessi's favorite meals for Friday evening, and Adam tries to arrange his schedule so that they can catch up on each other's lives. Their dinner conversations sometimes continue into the evening, as they talk about the books they've read, series they've streamed, podcasts they recommend, and what is happening with their friends. As part of the conversation, family members share their weekend plans. When they all have plans, Friday evening and church on Sunday may be the only time they are together.

If Jessi wants her parents' help on a school project, finances, or her car, she lets them know ahead of time. If she has brought laundry home, she takes care of it herself, and sometimes she and her dad take a walk before she returns to campus on Sunday afternoon.

"Rules of the road" are not uncommon when parents let their adult children remain at home.

Adam has a steady girlfriend, and his parents make her welcome in their home. Sometimes they take the couple out to eat. When Adam moved back home, his parents made it clear that they were happy to have him, and that they wanted to help him with an education or some kind of career training, whatever his choice. They also acknowledged that things would be different than it was when he was still in high school. His room would be his own, which meant that he would take responsibility for keeping it clean—to his satisfaction, not theirs. He was welcome to have guests over, but not overnight. (Someone they knew had found themselves running a free "boarding house" for their son's friends, and they did not want to get caught in that trap.)

Neal and Brenna have agreed that as long as Adam is in training, they will not charge him rent, though he pays for his own car insurance. If he chooses to continue living at home once he finishes school and gets a full-time job, he will begin paying rent. For now, his part-time job pays enough to cover his expenses. He and his folks make it a habit to eat together on Wednesday evenings, either at home or at a restaurant.

Such "rules of the road" are not uncommon when parents let their adult children remain at home. The rules may include policies regarding payment for rent and/or food and specific duties and expectations.

Neal and Brenna's home is not an empty nest, but neither is it a place of conflict. If they have a problem with Adam or he with them, they discuss it openly. In three years, they have had only two real conflicts and have resolved them in a friendly fashion. They all enjoy this "unempty nest" stage of life. The children often ask their parents' advice about school and also their relationships. Brenna and Neal feel that they are giving Adam and Jessi the freedom to develop their own independence and at the same time continuing to have a positive influence on them.

Del and Sherry's Story

Del and Sherry Peterson have a different sort of unempty nest with three children at home, and they too have managed to make it good for everyone.

Seventeen-year-old Jill is a junior in high school; she is interested in justice and social issues and is considering becoming a paralegal for a nonprofit. As of now, she expects to do her first two years of college while living at home, and then transfer to live on campus for her final two. Rick is nineteen and doesn't have a steady job. Ben at twenty-one is the assistant manager of a local store. Neither Rick nor Ben is interested in college.

Since graduating from high school, Rick has had three part-time jobs but quit each one to take a trip with his friends. He has no particular vocational interests; he does plan to work full-time someday but hopes it won't interfere too much with his routine.

Ben had worked in a grocery store during high school and became friends with the manager. After graduation he set his sights on becoming a store manager. Within three years he made assistant and is thoroughly excited about the possibilities for a productive future.

When Ben decided not to attend college, his parents were disappointed. Neither of them had gone and they hoped all their children would. When Rick, their second-born, announced that he also had no interest in college, his parents were more disturbed. Unlike Ben, he had not worked part-time during high school and after graduation, and it took him three months to find the first of his part-time jobs. With his record of quitting jobs, his parents were concerned about his future.

When Ben decided that he wanted to work toward becoming a store manager, Del and Sherry called the family together and invited him to explain his desires to the entire family. The conference included his career plans—his boss suggested he take a couple of courses at the community college. When he completed these, he would be ready to be promoted and earn a reasonable living, though he should keep the door open to further education in business management. The family meeting also included negotiations about continuing to live at home and how this would

"Isn't that part of what it means to be an adult? That you begin to pay your own way?"

impact the rest of the family. They discussed Ben's ongoing contribution toward family chores. Sherry had gone full-time at her job once Jill had started high school, and she was no longer as available to tend to the household as she had been previously.

When they came to the matter of finances, the family discussed whether or not Ben should pay rent or save up for a place of his own. "Isn't that part of what it means to be an adult?" Del asked. "That you begin to pay your own way?"

Ben agreed with his dad and said he preferred to pay something toward household finances, especially as he had a full-time job. His mom, Sherry, suggested that they begin by charging a relatively small amount that would increase each month until it reached the same level as if he had an apartment of his own. The assumption was that Ben could be saving up for his own place and that once he finished the recommended courses and was promoted at work, he'd be in better shape to move out and support himself.

Sherry had another concern about Ben's living at home, one especially important to her. "I'm afraid that if we agree that Ben can come and go as he pleases, I am going to be lying awake at night wondering where he is if he doesn't come in by, let's say, midnight. Being his mom, I just can't help it," she said. "I want him to have freedom to do what he wants to do, but I also want some peace of mind myself. Dad and I don't come and go without telling each other where we will be. Because we are part of the family, we let one another know if we are going to be late or if something unexpected arises. Part of being a loving family is that we do not cause each other concern."

Since that conference, Ben is still at home and is paying a fair amount monthly for rent and utilities. He's expecting to move out within a year. Their plan has worked well and neither he nor his parents have any complaints.

Ah, you say, *so a family conference with members agreeing to rules is part of the solution.* Yes, but a conference will not always satisfy everyone. As for the middle sibling, Rick, the situation was somewhat different and led to another family conference.

Although Del and Sherry were concerned about Rick's lack of direction, they understood his desire to travel, since they wished they had done this when they were younger, before more adult responsibilities set in. They agreed to one year for travel, after which Rick would go to school or get a job. He was also in a band that played at local events, which could keep him out late, and he'd sometimes spend the night at a friend's home. Sherry wanted to know where he was, and Rick agreed to contact her whenever he wouldn't be home for the night.

When they got to the subject of finances, they realized that playing gigs with a band wasn't generating the kind of income his brother Ben had started earning right out of high school. Rick felt he should not pay anything toward the household, yet his parents thought that he should pay a small amount of rent, just on principle. They also expected him to use the money he earned with the band for the traveling he wanted to do. His siblings Jill and Ben also agreed, though Ben noted that while traveling, paying rent would be difficult and unfair for his brother as he wasn't getting the benefits of home living.

The Petersons knew that one size does not fit all. After much discussion, their father said, "What if we say that when you are on a trip with your friends, you won't pay any rent. But when you are home, you will pay a minimal amount each month. That way you're making a contribution to the family."

Rick agreed to that and also to Jill's request that he do household chores when home. Then their father added, "I think we should understand that we are all agreeing to this for only one year. If you should decide to continue to live here after the year, then I think we will have to take a fresh look at all of this." Again, Rick agreed.

After one year of relative freedom, Rick began to consider what he would do. He'd long been computer-savvy and thinks he could land a job as a tech who repairs and restores computers. His parents feel quite comfortable that he will settle down and do well in whatever he chooses. Now that the year of travel is past, they have made it clear that it's time to either go to school for some kind of training or find full-time work. They are not open to him continuing to live at home for basically a token amount per month. If after he gets a job he wants to continue to live at home, they all agreed that the plan they followed with Ben would also be a workable plan with Rick.

Meanwhile, in another year Jill will begin at the community college. The family is committed to support her ambition to work for a nonprofit.

Del and Sherry are pleased with the relationships they have with their young adult children. They feel they have been successful in making this extended nesting period a productive time in their own lives and in the lives of their adult sons and soon-to-leave-the-nest daughter.

GUIDELINES FOR THE UNEMPTY NEST

These two families highlight several guidelines for relating to your young adult children still living at home. The foremost of these is that as a parent you *clarify expectations.* If you have one set of expectations and your older teenager or twentysomething has another, you are all setting yourselves up for a battle. But, if you can all agree on the expectations, you will be laying a foundation for a harmonious relationship now and in the future.

Here are five other guidelines for the parents and adult children who share a home:

1. Maintain open communication. You cannot clarify expectations without having open communication. The family conference illustrated by Del and Sherry provides an open forum where each family member can share ideas and feelings and together come to a consensus. If you have used this approach in earlier years, you know its benefit. If you have not, this is an excellent time to begin. In this type of open forum, you as parents need to listen carefully to the thoughts, feelings, and desires of your children. This does not mean that they have the final word, but that you take their opinions seriously.

2. Balance freedom and responsibility. Every parent is challenged to help the child find the proper balance between freedom and responsibility, since they are two sides of the same coin. In dealing with children who may not feel very much like adults yet, you need to keep in mind that you are all trying to arrive at appropriate guidelines. Certainly, emerging adults should be given more freedom than high school students, but freedom does not preclude responsibility. If they are to live at home, they must assume responsibilities for the welfare and peace of the family. These need to be made specific in areas of finance, chores, and common courtesies.

3. Honor your moral values. Moral values have to do with actions we believe to be right and wrong. Frequently the personal values of young adults differ from those of their parents. If your adult children plan to continue living at home, you have a right to ask them to continue to respect the values you as the parents adhere to. It is certainly appropriate for you to say that your children are not welcome to invite persons of the opposite sex to spend the night in their rooms. It is also appropriate to expect that your adult children will not use tobacco, alcohol, or drugs in your home if these are your values. In so doing, you are not forcing your personal values but expecting your children to respect your beliefs as long as they live with you. A kind but firm commitment to your own values demonstrates that you have strength of character.

4. Consider your own physical and mental health. When Sherry insisted that Ben and Rick let her know where they were late at night, she was protecting her own emotional health and well-being. She knew that she would lie awake worrying if she didn't know their whereabouts. Some parents are able to disconnect and let a young adult come and go as he pleases, while others are not. Most parents want to know when the adult child will return; otherwise, they worry for his or her safety. If that's your approach, set an appropriate rule that everyone lets others know when they will be back at night. You need to know your own limitations and take care of yourself responsibly. You cannot help or influence others if you don't first care for your own needs. This may even touch on the state of a grown child's room—sometimes closing the door is better than looking at a mess.

5. Set time limits and goals. When Del and Sherry agreed to allow Rick to travel and have a year of freedom after high school, they were letting him do something valuable but with a time limitation. Also, their agreement with Ben about paying increasing rent defined his financial responsibility to the family. Setting a goal regarding when the adult child will move out can give him motivation. The limits and situations vary. If he has an entry-level job, perhaps the family agrees he will move when he gets his first promotion. If your son or daughter is engaged to be married, they might stay at home until the wedding date. Often the parents and young adult find it easier to agree on a definite time limit, such as six months or a year. While goals and time limits may need to be renegotiated along the way, it is important to have them in place from the beginning.

DISORDER IN THE NEST

As you read about life in the Collier and Peterson households, you may have wondered, *Is it always this perfect? Where are the arguments? This isn't what happens in our house.* Certainly, ongoing nesting arrangements aren't always positive and enjoyable for everyone. You may be in an uneasy situation that you wish would end.

Remember these two words: **pleasant** *and* **firm**. *If you can be both pleasant and firm, you will get through the tough time without doing damage that you will have to apologize for or repair later.*

When parents and their young adult children share the same roof, tensions can develop for many reasons. The parents may feel they have lost their freedom, and the child may feel he is not respected as an adult. Both parent and child are adults with their own preferences. Each may have the desire to control. The kitchen, the living room, and the bedroom can all become battlefields. The television and the shower may become sources of irritation. This often leads to arguments. In fact, the primary complaint of most parents in your situation is that there is too much arguing in the home.

That may be true, and it does no good to assign blame for who's causing the arguments. More important is what you can do to reduce the arguing. Because your young adult child is still dependent on you, you may be tempted to respond to disagreements the same way you did when your child was much younger. You may say something like "I'm still in charge here. This is my house and I say how things are going to be!" This sort of response may sound and feel good at the time, but the result will not be positive in the long run. Being unpleasant to your child will get you nowhere. Dumping your resentment or anger on your child will cause him to resent you. This only provokes another argument.

When tensions escalate during an argument, you may be at a loss as to how to handle the situation. You may even feel so upset that you fear you will lose control and say something that will truly cause harm. And yet, you have to say or do something. Please remember these two words: *pleasant* and *firm*. If you can be both pleasant and firm, you will get through the tough time without doing damage that you will have to apologize for or repair later.

The most mature stance for parents is to *refuse to argue.* It is not always easy to gain enough self-control to do this, but it pays off in countless ways. The key is to listen to your child's side of a situation and then use "I" messages, which calm anger and invite understanding. A "you" message generally sounds accusatory and unpleasant. "You make me so angry when you do that!" An "I" message conveys your feelings and expectations but does not lay blame. "I feel so angry when you do that." No one can argue with how you feel. Such messages will help you remain pleasant but firm—and they will help your child understand what is causing your feelings of anger.

DEALING WITH ANGER

Remember that as a parent you have the greatest influence on your children, good or bad. The factor that has the most influence on them is the way you manage your anger. The way you manage your anger affects your children in several ways, for example: their self-esteem, sense of identity, ability to relate to other people, perceptions of the world, and ability to manage stress and function in society.

> "How serious is the offense? To have the same response to minor issues as one does for major issues is to mismanage one's anger."[4]

If you mismanage your anger, you can cause your children to develop attitudes that are passive-aggressive, anti-authority, and/or self-defeating.

When you manage your anger in a mature fashion, you give your children one of the most caring gifts there is—a potent example that will help them grow to their own maturity without the afflictions that so many adults struggle with today. It is wonderful to see your children develop into conscientious, energetic, motivated, and well-liked adults, but this process takes time. The way you handle your anger will have a tremendous influence on how well and how fast your children mature.

The reason that parental management of anger is so important is that children of all ages are sensitive toward their parents' anger. It is impossible for them to pass it off or to take it casually. Even one incident of mismanaged anger will cause extreme pain, just as mature handling of anger can intensify the love between parents and children. Every day you have a choice as to how you will handle your emotions in relation to your children. If you behave in a mature way, you will strengthen your bonds in the family.

Jim and Joan's Story

As we all know, we can be well-intentioned regarding our emotional reactions, and then be caught off guard by an unexpected turn of events. This is what happened to Jim and Joan McConnor and their only child, a nineteen-year-old daughter, Nina. When she graduated from high school, she decided to live at home while she attended college. She was accepted into a co-op program that offered her part-time work during college years and a good opportunity for employment after college.

Before Nina was far into her studies, her father began having acute difficulties at work. Jim's company was downsizing, and his job was on the line. This caused tension not only on the job but also at home. Though Joan was working, the prospect of reduced income and the uncertainty of Jim's future wore on them both. Now as the tension increased, Jim became more and more depressed, withdrawn, and anxious. As a result, he was very short with Nina and would frequently scold her for minor misunderstandings. He quickly went from being anxious to showing anger.

Nina withstood her father's unreasonable confrontations, but before long she dreaded coming home. When the home atmosphere worsened, Nina moved out of the house and roomed with a college classmate.

Because she wasn't ready for this financially or emotionally, she was unable to keep up with her work/study program. She became depressed and was not able to function well. Fortunately, Jim and Joan recognized their daughter's declining health and were able to get her and themselves into counseling, where they came to realize how they had failed their daughter. By this point, Jim had lost his job in the reorganization, but with his severance pay and Joan's income, they handled themselves well enough through it all and were able to give Nina the emotional support she needed. They persuaded her to move back home, and they worked at learning how to handle their anger and frustration in appropriate ways.

Nina said that two things helped her through this hard period. First, "My dad realized that I needed him. I also was sure that he still loved me." Despite his own agonies, Jim was able to keep her emotional love tank filled during that troubling time.

Second, Nina felt that her faith in God sustained her, especially when things were at their worst. Before Jim and Joan got the help they needed, Nina felt completely abandoned and alone, even in her prayers. But later she said, "God did answer, and He brought something wonderful out of a miserable situation. The Lord is very good at this sort of thing!"

TECHNIQUES FOR MANAGING ANGER

Everyone gets angry on a regular basis. Therefore, the question isn't whether you will become angry but how you will manage the emotion when it arises. The following suggestions for dealing with your feelings of anger will help you with your young adult children and also in other arenas of life.

First, *take responsibility*. The first step in managing anger is a willingness to be responsible for it. It is so easy to blame someone (or something) else for making you mad, and then to hold the person responsible for what the anger "made" you do or say. Unfortunately, many people use their anger as an excuse for whatever they want to justify. Consciously or unconsciously, they seek reasons to get angry so that they may excuse their own wrongdoing!

Before you can take responsibility for your anger, you need to identify it. Having been in both ministry and family counseling, I have often seen people who feel jealous, frustrated, or hurt and who are not aware that the basis of these feelings is anger. Although these people may not be aware of their anger, their children surely are. When parents refuse to identify and deal with their anger, their children feel less respect for them. However, when parents identify the anger, they are then able to name it and admit, "I am angry." Only then can they assume responsibility for it.

Blaming a child for your anger is self-defeating. It is also dangerous, because you will naturally blame her for other angers caused by totally unrelated situations. For example, you may have had an unresolved disagreement at work that you tried to put out of your mind. When you come home, your adult child's behavior upsets you. If you blame her for your anger, you may also unconsciously blame her for your earlier encounter at work. This sets you up to dump accumulated anger on the him or her. This tendency to dump anger is a common problem most parents have as a child emerges from a dependent state to a more self-sufficient state.

> "Blaming others rather than taking responsibility is a sign that you cannot manage your anger and the emotions that accompany each episode. Instead of being quick to blame another, take responsibility for your actions and feelings."[5]

Second, *remember the anger*. Because you don't feel proud of yourself when your anger gets out of control, it is easy to "forget" what happened. It is crucial to remember how you behaved, or you are later likely to unload your anger on someone else, or over suppress it and become passive-aggressive. So after your feelings subside, recall them. Remember your actions and their effect on others, as painful as that may be.

If this is a problem for you, try keeping a notebook of your progress in coping with anger. For instance, if someone treats you unfairly and you feel deeply hurt (angry), you may not be in a position to confront or deal with the hurt. But you can log the incident in your notebook and later record how you resolved the problem. The best way to handle the anger is verbally, pleasantly, and directly with the person you are angry at. If possible, you want to move toward reconciliation and greater understanding between you.

> "Often, our bodies are speaking what our minds are afraid to say, stories most of us have never had space to tell. The tales our bodies tell through our sensations reveal our deepest wounds, truths, and hopes."[6]

Third, *keep yourself healthy*. The better your general condition physically, spiritually, and emotionally, the more effective you will be in handling anger. Your body needs a balanced diet, and much information is readily available on nutrition and exercise in our body-conscious society. Millions of Americans are becoming increasingly overweight and out of shape, which can lead to depression and, in turn, anger. It is a vicious cycle that, when recognized, makes breaking the patterns you have acquired more doable.

Fourth, *use self-talk*. Even though you try to manage your anger well, at times you may lose it and risk dumping on your child. What then? One valuable technique is self-talk. Tell yourself something like, *I'm losing it. I don't want to make a fool of myself and say something I will later regret and have to apologize for. I'd better cool it!* If that doesn't do it, you might add, *I need to be and can be an example of a self-controlled adult, especially now that my children are older.*

If the self-talk doesn't calm you down, leave the room, start some chore—anything to get alone so that you can think about the situation and why you got so angry. It may help you to remember a funny or endearing incident involving your child when he was younger, one that will bring up pleasant feelings. What you are really doing is taking a time-out, just as you had your child do when he was small.

Fifth, *ask forgiveness*. If you have said or done something that you regret, you have a great opportunity to let good arise from a bad scene. The simple but difficult act of asking your adult child's forgiveness puts your relationship back on a loving basis. Regardless of the immediate response, this act enhances the child's respect for you and teaches your child the importance of forgiving others and oneself.

Since you got into the conflict in the first place, don't be afraid to constructively resolve it by asking for forgiveness and then moving toward a better relationship. Never forget that true intimacy comes from resolved conflict.

You can bring good from your painful encounters as you and your adult child move toward greater maturity and understanding.

four

When Your Child Moves Back Home

You may have seen the T-shirt that says, "It's not an empty nest until they get their stuff out of the attic." For you that may not seem even remotely funny. You aren't thinking about emptying the attic but about how you are going to manage when your child moves himself and all his things back into your house and life.

Greg and Shiran Mitchell knew this all too well. As Shiran explained to Dr. Braun, a family therapist they were seeing for the first time, "This is the last place we ever thought we would be. And to get Greg here is a near miracle!" Her husband nodded sheepishly and then explained why they had come to the counselor.

"Our kids have always done fairly well. No serious problems—just the usual stuff. After they finished college, we thought our parenting days were essentially over, but were we ever wrong! Our second child, Nick, graduated from a good university and was ready to get out on his own, or so we thought. He took temporary jobs and lived with friends for nearly a year while he was looking for a position related to his field of study. When that didn't happen, he became discouraged and asked if he could move back home."

"What could we say?" continued Shiran. "He just wasn't making it out there. He felt like a failure and seemed to lose all motivation. We had never seen him that way before and so we let him come home. However, that made us wonder if we hadn't done a good job as parents. Nick has been home now for three months and just sits around the house. One day we think maybe we should just let him rest and recover and the next day we feel like wringing his neck and pushing him out the door. We're up and down emotionally, but mostly down—worried, frustrated, scared."

"Whenever we talk to him about it," said Greg, "he just looks at us with forlorn eyes and tries to be agreeable, saying something like, 'I'm trying, Dad,' or agreeing with whatever we say. Then he goes off to listen to podcasts or scroll through his phone. He hasn't even looked for a job except online in the usual places."

Dr. Braun asked the Mitchells to describe Nick's high school and college experiences.

"He was always an easygoing kid who kept up with his friends. He was active in sports and church youth group activities," Shiran said. "He got above-average grades without studying too much. He seemed to feel reluctant to leave home for college but soon adjusted to life there. He did fairly well in college, was involved in some activities, and dated now and then, but nothing serious. He graduated with a degree in English, not knowing what he wanted to do, but that's not too unusual. I guess he figured something would just pop up. When it didn't, he asked to move home. Tell us, did we do something wrong as parents?"

Before Dr. Braun could answer, Greg asked his own question: "Why isn't he out there doing his thing? When we were his age, we couldn't wait to get away from home and make our own way. What's wrong with him? I know it costs a lot to live, but still ... maybe we did too much for him. Maybe we didn't teach him to be responsible," Greg went on.

Shiran leaned toward her husband and said, "Now, don't blame yourself. We need help for Nick; that's why we're here."

"But we've hardly gotten started. We haven't told Dr. Braun about Noelle."

"She's older than Nick?"

"Yes, she's twenty-eight and has a three-year-old daughter," Greg explained. "Last week she and little Ava moved home, and this is what really prompted us to seek some help. Her husband was killed in a traffic accident a few months ago, and

> **"What would happen if you said this to yourself the next time you remember a mistake? *I wasn't perfect, for sure. We all make mistakes, so I'm going to give myself grace and move on.*"**[1]

there wasn't enough insurance for her to keep the home. So she sold the house and needs our help for a while."

Shiran picked up the story. "She was always very responsible, did well in school, got an associate's degree and certified as a dental hygienist. However, she has worked only part-time for the last four years and feels that she needs a few more courses to keep up with the changes in her profession. We understand her situation and are glad to help her. What we don't understand is our own reactions. We dearly love our granddaughter, but we hadn't counted on taking care of her this much, or on having our two children back home at this time in our lives."

————

You may know a Nick and a Noelle in your home or just down the street, for their numbers are increasing. It isn't the fact of two generations or more living in the same house that causes a problem, but the unexpectedness of the return home. Parents thought their son or daughter had left home and were living independently for good, but then . . . they come back.

Responding to Their Return

As Greg and Shiran learned, their main problem was not the return of the children but their own reactions and uncertainties. After they were able to better understand themselves and also work out practical ways to deal with Nick and Noelle, their anxieties lessened. The parents and the two adult children were all able to enjoy this unexpected time together again, and now with Ava too.

After Greg and Shiran had met with Dr. Braun a couple of times, they told Nick that they wanted him to come along with them to a session, since what they were discussing involved the entire family. When he resisted, they used the leverage they had hesitated to use before and told him that since he was living there, he needed to work toward a solution of the problem that sent them to the counselor in the first place. When Nick realized he didn't have much choice, he accompanied his parents.

To his surprise, Nick found the conversations helpful in better understanding his own fears and lethargy and also in understanding his parents' point of view. The three of them sat down and worked out first steps of a plan. They started at the three-month mark: within that timeframe, Nick would be working full-time, even if it wasn't the career of his dreams. He agreed he would take something, just to be working and contribute to the household. He also agreed to shop for groceries and be responsible for suppers twice a week as well as do his own laundry and take part in other regular chores. After three months, they would reevaluate the situation and see what the next steps were. Greg and Shiran wrote up this agreement and the three of them signed and dated it, showing Nick that they were treating him as an adult and depending on him to keep up his end of the bargain.

It wasn't long before Nick began sincerely looking for a job. With his degree in English, he found a job as a feature reporter for a local newspaper. It didn't pay too well, so he supplemented his income at a gourmet coffee shop and soon felt the self-satisfaction of earning a living. He confided to his parents he had always wanted to be a political cartoonist and hoped his role at the newspaper might lead to something in that field. If Greg and Shiran thought that goal was a bit narrow and improbable, they did not say so. They were pleased that Nick was giving serious thought to what he wanted to do in the future.

Since Noelle's move home was beyond her control and was to be for a limited time, and since she was pursuing advanced training to enable her to advance in her field of dental hygienics, Shiran and Greg decided to relax and just enjoy the time with their granddaughter.

Responding to Emotional Issues

Grown children return home for several reasons—some practical and financial, but some emotional. And there are times when parents have reason to be concerned about the emotional health of their children who bring with them the scars from their unsuccessful attempts at making it in the adult world . . . such as Stephanie.

At age twenty-nine, Stephanie returned home, her self-confidence shattered by her experiences of the last ten years. Her father, Will, told Dana Roberts, the counselor he contacted, "We have a serious problem on our hands. Stephanie has returned home with real emotional problems, and we don't know how to help her. We don't mind her living with us for a while, but we know this isn't good for her in the long run."

Dana Roberts agreed to see Stephanie. When she came to the appointment, Dana saw that the young woman was very self-effacing and tried to put her at ease. "Call me Dana," she said with a smile. Stephanie apologized for being late, even though she was two minutes early. During the conversation, she said "I'm sorry" numerous times, apologized for taking up her time, for crying, for needing a tissue.

Stephanie's ten-year journey from the nest and back had been mostly a downhill slide with only a few intervals of temporary excitement. She remembered the thrill of going off to college, but she remembered even more deeply the lonely weekends when other girls were dating, and she was in her room or in the library. She made good enough grades and was commended by her professors, but she had few friends.

Stephanie earned her bachelor's degree in economics, and soon after college got a job in the business office of a local company, a medium-sized firm that specialized in custom-built residential and commercial doors. She moved into her own apartment. Her work went well, but she had little social contact. Then she became active in the singles program of a large church where she attended social occasions and participated in service projects with the group. She dated some, but no relationship lasted long before going flat.

Then she became good friends with Marti, and the two decided to live together and share expenses. This was a happy period in Stephanie's life, since the two women had many common interests. "We really enjoyed being with each other," Stephanie told Dana. "But Marti began dating seriously the next year and, of course, we spent less time together doing things. A year later, she got married and moved out of town. I really was happy for her, but it hurt me. I felt a sense of loss when she left."

As she talked, the counselor determined Stephanie felt depressed. Others in the church group had tried to encourage her by inviting her to various events, but her depressive behavior pushed them away. Finally, she dropped out of the group.

Her depression also affected her work to the point that her boss suggested that perhaps she should look for another job. This was the last straw for Stephanie, since the job had been her one place of stability and achievement. "I felt like such a failure. Three months later they let me go. I just didn't have the heart to look for another job, so I asked my parents if I could move back home."

In promptly seeking help, her father was admitting his own limitations. This is an important step in responding to our children who are struggling emotionally.

Stephanie is typical of many adult children who return home the worse for wear. Their experience in the adult world has depleted their emotional energy, and their psychological and physical problems motivate them to retreat from life rather than pursue a vision.

Parents who open their doors to these tired children are often tired themselves. They don't have the skills to cope with their young adult children, and in an attempt to do so, they often become frustrated and depressed.

Will, Stephanie's father, acted responsibly when he reached out for help within a few weeks of her return home. He and his wife were willing to provide her a place to stay, but they were unable to deal with her emotional and social problems. In promptly seeking help, he was admitting his own limitations. This is an important step in responding to our children who are struggling emotionally. Many parents fail to take action, hoping that their child will soon regain emotional composure and reenter the adult world of independent living. Months can drag into years of his or her becoming more dependent.

For Stephanie, help thankfully came sooner than later. In addition to providing counseling for her and her parents, Dana was able to get her enrolled in a class on building self-esteem where she learned some valuable concepts and also found new acquaintances. When the class ended, she took another on building relationship skills. In this one, she learned why she had been unable to form long-term relationships in the past. With the help of the group and individual counseling, she was able to correct many behavior patterns that were barriers in her social contacts.

Within three months of returning home, Stephanie had another job, and nine months later she moved into an apartment that she would share with another young woman. Her depression had lifted, and she was excited about the possibilities of the future. That was five years ago. Today, Stephanie is enjoying a position in human resources for a home-improvement chain. She joined a book discussion group through the library where she has made new friends, both men and women. She looks back on the year she spent with her parents as a critical turning point, a time in which she dealt with problems she had never faced before and took personal steps of growth to overcome destructive personality patterns. She's enjoying her present life and optimistic about the future.

PLANNERS AND STRUGGLERS

Planners intend to spend the time at home in preparation. Their rationale usually includes saving money, paying school debts, and building a nest egg for the future. They see their parents' home as a sheltered and inexpensive environment while they seek the perfect job and or perhaps a spouse.

Yes, these people may seem to be maturing slowly, but the planners are usually savvy in the way they use their resources to their advantage, often without being a burden to their families. Even if they don't hit the right career track right away, they are still working, and many of them contribute to household expenses.

Evidence indicates that planners generally do well in moving home and preparing themselves financially and socially for a secure future. They add vitality to their parents' lives, and their relationships with family usually thrive and deepen with mutual respect and understanding.

Strugglers tend to return home out of necessity. Their plans go no further than "living at home for a while." They find the outside world threatening and don't want to struggle on their own. They do not see the world as a friendly, welcoming place, and do not want to leave the security of home. They are simply not ready for the intense competition and rapid change of today's society.

Young adults who are strugglers have many motivations. Most of them are capable adults who are just slow in their maturational process. If they are handled well by their parents, they will reach the level of maturity necessary to go out on their own and lead productive and meaningful lives. They simply need more time in the nest. Parents who can respond with understanding will later be delighted and overwhelmingly proud when their children become independent adults.

UPSIDES OF HAVING A RETURNER

Parents who have adult children at home can consider themselves fortunate in several ways. First, they are able to help their children; many parents lose close contact with them. Parents of strugglers also have the opportunity to rectify past mistakes and to escape the dreadful feelings of guilt that plague many parents, sometimes for the rest of their lives. With these returning children, parents can form new bonds of love and affection while strengthening old ones; this can create some of the most meaningful memories between parents and children.

Another positive is that parents have additional time with their children while the children are developing life's values. For example, twenty-two-year-old Nelson has returned home having spent four years in college, but without completing his degree. He is now looking for work and wondering what to write on job applications: "graduated from college" or "attended college"? *Won't the latter raise unnecessary questions in the mind of the hiring manager? Will the employer actually check my college records?* These questions of expedience versus integrity race through Nelson's mind, and he decides to discuss the issue with his parents. His parents have the opportunity to help their son consider the importance of integrity. At this crucial stage in his life, their influence can affect his success or failure for years to come. If he were not living with his parents, Nelson may never have discussed the issue with them, and they would not have had this opportunity.

Most strugglers who come home need emotional support, and this can place their parents in a difficult role. The strugglers have met with failure or experiences they could not handle. They are hurting and need love and support. As parents we must remind ourselves that we *all* need our parents' love and support. After a parent dies, we need the memory of their care and love.

In a time of stress, it is easy to forget these truths. When a struggler returns home, we must not lose the overall picture of family ties over a lifetime. If we fulfill our parental duties to the best of our ability, we will see our adult child heal, recover, and fly again. At the time, it may seem like a nightmare, and we may become exasperated as we watch our own offspring appear to fail. Yet, we can also see it as a wonderful opportunity. The future is not dark. Our adult child will heal, regain their strength, and try again.

A Harris survey found that 40 percent of young people who moved back home reported feeling happy to be there, while 33 percent said they felt smart for making the choice to live with family.[2]

LOVING AND CHALLENGING

When an adult child is experiencing hardship, disappointment, and pain, the way her family and loved ones treat her will make the difference in the character she develops. If she is treated with respect and love, encouragement and support, she will eventually come out of the difficult days a more mature and capable person. But if parents treat her with dismay, frustration, and anger, she will suffer even more and most likely become a bitter person with more pain to overcome.

Parents need to maintain a balance as they seek to help. First, they should offer support in their love, encouragement, and perhaps financial help. And second, they should challenge their son or daughter to assume responsibility for herself and become an independent person. Because challenging the adult child can be difficult to negotiate, here are some guidelines for getting through this season successfully. It is important that parents and the adult child come to agreement about these items. Here are some ways to be loving yet challenging to your adult child:

1. Establish a time limit for the nesting experience. This does not have to be totally rigid or inflexible but there should be some sense of how long the arrangement will last. Everyone will feel more relaxed if they know there is a time limit.

2. If your child has returned while looking for their dream job, let them know they might need to take on something else in the meantime: fast food, temporary office work, seasonal construction; whatever it takes to meet their obligations, e.g., a phone bill, car payment.

3. Decide on an agreement that will take into account the financial goals and situations of all parties, as well as the expectations of all. In the rare event that a young person cannot make any financial contribution to the household, he can make other contributions, such as cleaning, yard work, repairs—anything that will aid the household.

4. It does not hurt to put an agreement in writing. This will help both parents and grown children understand the expectation on both sides. If they do not hold up their end, let them know they'll have one reminder and after that a month or whatever you mutually decide to make other arrangements.

5. Respect the need for privacy. The amount of privacy people need varies greatly, and this difference can become a source of friction and misunderstanding. This is an area in which open communication pays big dividends.

WHEN THEY BRING THEIR CHILDREN

Often children return home bringing their own children. When this happens, their parents' stress level may skyrocket. Not only do they face the pressures of dealing with their children, but they have the logistical and emotional struggles of caring for grandchildren. Darnell and Molly found themselves in this situation. When their daughter Beth returned with two young children, she told her parents that her husband had been physically and emotionally abusive for the past five years and now had left her for a woman he met at work. Beth was furious not only with her husband, Stan, but was disappointed with herself for allowing herself to have been abused for so long.

Her children were bewildered at what had happened to their daddy. They were excited about staying with their grandparents, but they often asked, "When is Daddy coming?"

Darnell and Molly opened their doors and their hearts to Beth and her children. They knew this was going to cause a radical change in their lifestyle, but they saw no alternative at the moment. They were not in a financial condition to rent an apartment for Beth; also, they knew that she needed their emotional support during this crisis.

During the first week Beth was there, her parents suggested that the three of them sit down and talk about the situation and decide on a strategy. Darnell began by saying, "Beth, I want you to know that we want to do everything we can to help you through this crisis. We know that this isn't what you wanted, but it's where we all are and we have to deal with it. If we're going to be successful in coming through this tough time, we have to work together as a team. Why don't we begin by making a list of the areas we'll need to deal with in the coming months?"

Together they made the following list:

Child care
The children's physical and emotional health
Food preparation
Finances
Beth's emotional health
Legal matters related to her husband
Darnell's and Molly's emotional health

"There are probably other things, but that's enough to confront now. Let's take the ones that seem most urgent and then talk about the others next week," Darnell suggested. "What is most pressing on your mind, Beth?"

"It all runs together for me. I know that I must take care of the children, and that's a full-time job. I also feel strongly that Stan needs to be held accountable for his actions. He needs to pay regular child support to help us financially. I guess those are the two biggest things on my mind now."

"Then let's discuss those two today," suggested her father.

They agreed that in the coming week they would find a lawyer for Beth so that she could begin the process of holding Stan accountable for helping the family. They also agreed that Beth should get some counseling to help her process her emotions. Molly, who had a part-time job at the library each morning, would be willing to keep the children on the afternoons that Beth needed to be involved in legal proceedings or with the counselor.

For the next several weeks, they continued to have family conferences dealing with various aspects of their life together and one by one worked out agreements for handling the logistics. Three months into the process, they decided that within a year Beth should plan to have her own apartment with the children and also a part-time job. With this income and the money she hoped to receive from Stan, she could be self-supporting.

Fifteen months later, Beth was able to move into her own place. She had found a job that she could do from her home. The children went to preschool each morning, and Darnell and Molly agreed to keep the children two nights a week to give Beth a break.

COMMUNITY RESOURCES

When struggling adult children return home, many parents are not able to manage the problems alone. It is important to be open to finding and using services offered by people in the community. Counselors, ministers, and physicians all stand ready to give individual attention. Local colleges, social groups, libraries, churches, and other organizations often sponsor activities designed to give practical help to those struggling with emotional, financial, or physical difficulties. Parents who encourage their returned children to take advantage of these resources provide a great service for their young people and also for themselves.

When There Are Special Needs

Finding resources is particularly important in families having children with some form of handicap. Adult children with disabilities pose special challenges and may never be able to leave home. This ongoing experience for parents can be draining. Their children need continuing help, but so do they.

In addition to the many professional people in the community whose job it is to serve such families, most churches are willing to help, if they know how and when. The parents are the ones who know best what would serve their family, and they should feel free to make reasonable suggestions to the appropriate persons at their churches. We have all read uplifting stories of "other-abled" individuals who are vitally involved with people in their neighborhoods, but such involvement has to be coordinated by a caring person, usually a parent, who enlists the help of those who want to serve.

If this isn't your situation but you know of families who do have these needs, consider finding out what you can do to give them some help: stay with the child while the parents run errands or just go out for an evening; celebrate birthdays and milestones; bring coffee and a snack over and visit; accept that you can't understand everything about their lives; find a church that has a disability ministry and help your friend get there.

WHEN IT'S TIME TO SAY GOODBYE

When children return home, parents need to remember that they are adults and ultimately responsible for their own lives. All the planning and goals and support and resources available will not do the job if the young person isn't amenable to change. If they choose to walk away from parental love and support, they have that freedom.

However, in some cases they don't walk away; instead, they stay too long. When it's time to move on but the young adult refuses to leave, his parents are in a difficult position. They know he is able to take care of himself; he seems to have recovered from his bad experiences and is generally pleasant. Yet he refuses to take responsibility for himself.

Devon was still living at home at twenty-eight. He had spent his college years studying minimally, making poor to fair grades, and had not graduated. He got excited for a while about learning a trade, took a few courses, and then lost interest. Although he was capable of excellent work, he always seemed to find ways of failing to meet the expectations of parents and teachers alike. He was friendly and had friends, but as his friends were moving ahead with adult life and he wasn't, Devon started drifting away from these relationships.

His parents finally insisted that the three of them go for family counseling. After two sessions, it became evident that Devon was not going to cooperate or attempt to become a self-sufficient person. His father, Wes, wanted to insist he leave home, but his mother, Lacy, was unwilling to be that "cruel."

At times, parents will have to act, giving a deadline and then enforcing it by asking the adult child to leave the home for his own welfare. This is love—tough but true love—in action. Often this action can be preceded by the help of a counselor, pastor, or another third party.

Devon refused to continue going with his parents to counseling, so Wes and Lacy went alone. With the counselor's help, they developed a plan that satisfied Wes's need to take action and Lacy's need to be gentle though firm.

Devon's parents laid out the plan for him. They would set him up in an apartment and pay his living expenses for six months. After that time, they would decrease the support so that he would be on his own six months later. Although this was risky, Wes and Lacy felt that they had no other option.

Devon was livid and began to accuse them. "You really don't care about me! I'll never forgive you for this. You'll be sorry!" His anger nearly caused Lacy to back down, but she was finally able to see that Devon's response indicated that he really did need to learn some real-world lessons, just like everyone else.

When his anger didn't work, Devon tried to negotiate with his parents, promising that he would take more responsibility, if he could just stay at home. Wes reminded him that he had said those same words at other times, but without honoring them. All of this was very difficult for Lacy, but deep down she knew that their plan was best for their son.

When he saw that he had no other options, Devon moved out. And gradually he changed. He found employment that would meet his financial obligations if he trimmed his lifestyle. Eventually he learned to be responsible for his way of life. His relationship with his parents still went through some rocky times, but now he is thankful to his parents for being firm with him.

LOVING OUR RETURNING KIDS

As you well know, adult children can present you with a wide variety of challenging situations that call for adaptability, imagination, innovation, firmness, love, and every other skill you ever learned in your many years of parenting. You met the challenges of the past and you have to believe that you can also meet the ones confronting you today. The goal is to move your children to maturity and to let them eventually be free of the home nest, out on their own.

Most adult children who have returned home respond positively to the love and encouragement of their parents. They are at a point of crisis and know they need help. They have returned to the one source where they believe they can receive such help. As they and you keep the future in mind, you can all proceed with optimism. You and your children are going to be connected in vital ways as long as you all live; you want to move toward their future, and your own, with skillful and loving care that offers promise of what you all want most.

five

When Well-Meaning Isn't Enough

Most any parent will tell you: parenting has wonderful rewards, but it also requires an exacting price. This price may be logistical or practical, as we saw in the chapters about grown children staying in or moving back to the family home. The price may also be emotional, as we observe our adult children struggling.

As parents, we want our children to reach the point where they can function independently of us. We want this for their own good and also for ours, since we have been through many years of the hard work of parenting and now desire the freedom that comes with the children having grown up. It's our time to enjoy the fruit of our labors and watch our children follow their own dreams while we explore new horizons for ourselves. It is the way life is designed—children are born to become adults.

If all goes well, we will encourage our children through the uncertain years of young adolescence, watch them grow in self-confidence through their high school years, reach out to pursue education or

> An old saying goes, "Small children, small problems. Big children, big problems."

vocation, eventually be self-supporting, perhaps have a family, and continue to relate to us in a positive but somewhat less intense manner.

However, in contemporary Western culture, it is a common story for an adult child to have a history of doing well in life up to a certain point and then begin to have problems that cripple him to the point of devastation. In this chapter, we'll discuss some of these more serious problems. Most adult children in similar predicaments can receive the help they need and go on to enjoy a happy and productive life, as most of the problems are treatable, if they are identified and worked through.

Since parents are usually the ones observing their children most closely, they tend to know when something is beyond the range of ordinary and needing professional help. And yet, many hesitate, because they do not know the signs by which to identify potentially serious problems. In this chapter I'll discuss some of the most common hurdles to independence—depression, passive-aggressive behavior, substance abuse, attention-deficit/hyperactivity disorder (ADHD)—and offer guidance, encouraging you toward the goal: to bring your children to maturity and independence.

DEPRESSION

Depression is the most common problem that can harm or destroy a young person's life. Not only is it a malady in itself, but it complicates all other difficulties. Remember Stephanie, who fell into a depression when her roommate left and she felt she had no friends? Her work suffered and eventually she felt like a complete failure.

Although depression today is better understood than it once was, it is still one of the most unrecognized causes of problems in young adults. Depression in young adults is similar to adolescent depression, and that makes it complex, subtle, and dangerous. It is complex because of its many intricate causes and effects. It is subtle because it almost always goes undetected, even by the young person, until a crisis occurs. It is dangerous because depression can result in the worst of happenings—anything from work failure to suicide.

Causes of Depression

It is also important for parents to realize that there are different kinds of depression and that they come from several causes. Depression may have a physical cause. Also, it may be situational or reactive, in that it grows out of a painful situation in life. Such depression is a reaction to difficult experiences, especially those that involve loss. For example, depression often follows the loss of a spouse by divorce, the loss of a job, the loss of a parent to death, the loss of a friendship, or the loss of money. Depression may also arise over the loss of a dream.

Another form of depression is rooted in a biochemical disorder that puts the mind and emotions in a state of disequilibrium. This is sometimes referred to as endogenous depression, meaning "from within the body." Depression can be a biochemical and neurohormonal process, affecting the body's blood chemistry and hormones, and this kind usually develops slowly.

The good news about biologically caused depression, which accounts for about a third of all cases, is that it is treatable with medication. But situational depressions are more common, and medications are of limited value in treating these, unless they have gone on for a long time and have affected the body's biochemistry.

Severity of Depression

In this age group of young adults, depression is hard to identify because its symptoms are different from the classic symptoms of depression in adults who are a little older. For example, a young adult in mild depression usually acts and talks normally and displays no outward symptoms. Mild depression is manifested in depressing fantasies, daydreams, or in dreams during sleep. It is detectable only by knowing the person's thought patterns and thought content. Not many professionals can identify depression at this stage.

The mental and physical pain at this stage can be excruciating, even unbearable; yet the young adult will still try to cover up his or her depression.

The young adult in moderate depression acts and talks normally. However, the content of his speech is affected, as he dwells primarily on subjects such as death, morbid problems, and crises. Since many adults today seem to dwell on pessimistic trains of thought, your grown child's depression may go unnoticed.

Moderate depression in the young adult is just as profound and serious as moderate depression in the older adult. Biochemically and neurohormonally, the two are identical, but the manifestations and symptoms are usually different. A moderately depressed older adult looks terrible, feels miserable, and is severely affected in his ability to function. At the same level, the young adult does not appear depressed. Therefore, when a young adult seems to others to be extremely depressed, we need to assume that he is profoundly depressed and in real trouble.

If the depression deepens, a severe depression can develop. The mental and physical pain at this stage can be excruciating, even unbearable; yet the young adult will still try to cover up his or her depression. But there are certain telltale signs, which we will discuss shortly.

One reason depression is difficult to identify in young adults is that they are good at masking it. They can cover it by appearing to be all right, even when they are absolutely miserable. This condition is often called "smiling depression." Young people unconsciously employ this front, especially when other people are around. They might not want anyone to know of the struggle for various reasons: worry about others' reaction, unwillingness to burden their family and friends, not wanting an employer to know there's a problem, not realizing they should seek help or not knowing how to do so.[1]

But when they're alone they let down the mask somewhat. This letdown is helpful to parents, especially if the child is living in the home, or if they're in their company regularly and thus are able to observe their children's countenance. The transformation in the face is amazing; when they are alone, they appear terribly sad and miserable. As soon as they think someone is watching, they don they smiling mask.

> —
> Individuals with smiling depression often look happy to the outside world and keep their depression a secret."[2]
> —

As a concerned parent, you will want to know how you can discover depression in your child so that you can do something about it before a tragedy occurs. A depressed young adult is quite susceptible to unhealthy peer pressure, and is prone to fall victim to drugs, alcohol, inappropriate sexual experiences, and other self-destructive behaviors.

Symptoms of Young Adult Depression

The best way for parents to identify depression is to recognize its symptoms and how those symptoms develop. It is crucial to be aware of all symptoms, since one or two may or may not signify actual clinical depression.

A depressed young adult will usually have at least one of the symptoms of older adults. These include emotions such as helplessness, persistent sadness, hopelessness, emptiness, despondency, and despair; withdrawal from others; and physical issues such as problems with sleep (either too much or too little); problems with eating—too much or too little, with weight loss; and lack of energy. Other symptoms can be feelings of low self-esteem and difficulties handling anger. It is important to remember that depression can cause anger.

Now, let's look at specific symptoms of depression in the young adult:

- **Shortened attention span.** In mild depression, the first symptom generally seen is a shortening of attention span. The person is unable to keep his mind focused on a subject as long as he once could; as his mind drifts from what he wants to focus on, he becomes increasingly distracted. This shortening of the attention span usually becomes obvious when he attempts to do detailed work or read complex material. He finds it harder to keep his mind on the subject, and the harder he tries, the less he accomplishes. Of course, this leads to frustration, as he blames himself for being stupid. He assumes that he does not have the intellectual ability for the task, and this is damaging to his self-esteem.

- **Daydreaming.** The shortened attention span affects the adult child at work. At the beginning of the day, she may be able to pay attention, but as the day goes on, her short attention span becomes more noticeable. As her depression deepens over time and the attention span shortens, her daydreaming increases. Unfortunately, this is usually interpreted as laziness or poor attitude.

- **Poor work performance.** As the attention span shortens and day-dreaming increases, the result is poor performance at work. Naturally the person's self-esteem suffers, which causes the depression to deepen even further.

- **Boredom.** As the young adult daydreams more and more, he gradually falls into a state of boredom. This usually manifests itself in his wanting to be alone for increasingly long periods of time. He also loses interest in things he once enjoyed.

- **Somatic symptoms.** As the boredom continues and deepens, the adult child gradually slips into moderate depression. At this point, she begins to suffer from *somatic depression*, that is, bodily depression. We use this term because even though depression is physiological or has a biochemical-neurohormonal basis at this point, the symptoms begin to affect the person in a directly physical way. For example, in moderate depression, the young adult begins to experience physical pain. This may occur in many places but is most often felt in the lower mid-chest region or as headaches.

- **Withdrawal.** In this miserable state, the person may withdraw from everyone, including friends. And, to make matters worse, she doesn't simply avoid her friends, but may disengage herself from them with such hostility, belligerence, and unpleasantness that she alienates them. As a result, she becomes very lonely.

Once prolonged boredom has set in, other symptoms can develop. A young adult in severe depression cannot tolerate his misery indefinitely and eventually becomes desperate enough to do something about it. At this point, drug or alcohol abuse may occur, or sexual adventures or sexual fantasies through pornography. Some will become increasingly involved with an anonymous online community or develop an unhealthy obsession with online gaming. Complete withdrawal from others is one telltale sign of severe depression.

Most amazing at this point is that many young adults are hardly aware that what they're going through is actually depression. Their ability to hide behind denial is truly incredible. This is the reason that others seldom suspect their friend—or child—is depressed until tragedy occurs.

Moderate to severe depression is not something you can consider a "phase" that will run its course. This insidious affliction tends to grow worse and worse unless the depression is identified and intervention is taken.

The struggler is more likely to be affected by depression than the planner, but depression can occur with any adult child. When it happens to young adults, it can affect their chances of making a start in the world, getting into satisfying activities, making friends, finding a compatible spouse. It is often an underlying reason why an adult child returns home.

At one time or another, depression affects millions of people in the United States—a Gallup poll reports a growing number of American adults as having been at some time or currently are experiencing depression.[3] Parents must be able to recognize the symptoms of depression if they wish to help their children.

HELPING WHEN YOUR ADULT CHILD IS DEPRESSED

Foster Communication

What can a parent do if a child is depressed? The first thing, of course, is to identify depression before it becomes severe. Once it is identified, parents can do much to help, even though they are in a difficult position, as most depressed persons are not open to communicating.

With this inherent hesitancy, the parents must try to keep open or reestablish the lines of communication. Badgering someone with questions is usually an exercise in futility; trying to get her to talk may increase her defensiveness.

So, what can you do to foster communication? If your son or daughter is content to be in the same room with you, as you both read or work on your laptops, you are fortunate. Simply being in the vicinity of someone who is depressed is a form of communication. It

Use "I" messages such as, "I hope I'm not imposing, but I would like you to know of my concern for you." Such a statement has the best chance to be taken positively and get a favorable response.

gives you the advantage of taking your time and making sure that you do nothing to cause her to put up more defenses. You can wait until your child takes the initiative to open or continue communication. It is good to let her bring up what is on her mind, what is troubling her. When this happens, you can offer suggestions about the underlying depression. It is best to approach this rather delicate subject when your child asks for your opinion. Most adults are touchy about their mental and emotional health and will accept suggestions only when they ask for them. If you have a good enough relationship to be able to be near your adult child at times when she is relaxed, you are in a good position to talk to her about your concerns when she is ready.

If such an opportunity does not present itself, you may wish to create one. One possibility is to take your child on a trip or some venture where you will naturally spend time together. Even if your child doesn't broach the subject, you may bring it up, using "I" messages such as, "I hope I'm not imposing, but I would like you to know of my concern for you." Such a statement has the best chance to be taken positively and get a favorable response.

Your child may respond with slight hostility—for instance, "What do you mean?" If she does, you can still continue the conversation. As long as you remain pleasant and soft-spoken, the interchange will continue until she understands that you care about her happiness and are worried that she may be depressed.

The main reason you want to be so careful about the way you approach your child regarding her depression is that you don't want her to misinterpret what you are saying. Also, you want to elicit her cooperation in finding help. This may be in the form of a competent counselor, the use of an antidepressant medication prescribed by a doctor, making constructive life changes, or all of these. The important thing is to maintain a positive relationship with your child during this difficult time.

Recognize the Dos and Don'ts of Depression

Depression has not always been accepted or understood. *What's she got to be depressed about?* or *Quit the pity party* have unfortunately been typical responses in some circles. Thankfully today we have more understanding of this condition and how to approach it. As a parent, whether or not you have experienced depression yourself, you can educate yourself and learn how to guide your adult child. Most parents are not able to give their children the kind of specialized help they need, but when professional assistance is needed, you can encourage your child to avail himself of this kind of help. As parents are in this delicate position of urging without pushing, they may be guided by the following suggestions:

Don'ts

- Don't tell him that he has nothing to be depressed about.
- Don't tell him that everything is going to be okay.
- Don't tell him to snap out of it or pull himself together.
- Don't tell her that the problem is spiritual.
- Don't tell her that the problem stems from her past failures.
- Don't tell her why you think she is depressed.
- Don't give advice; rather, encourage her to listen to her counselor.

Dos

- Do tell him that you are glad he is going for counseling.
- Do let him know that if he wants to talk, you want to listen.
- Do receive his feelings without condemning them. If he says, "I'm feeling empty," your response might be, "Would you like to tell me about it?"

- Do look for life-threatening symptoms such as suicidal talk or actions.

- Do inform the counselor of such talk.

- Do tell her that you believe in her and know she will come out of this. She should have hope that she will not always feel this way.

- Do encourage her to make decisions, but don't force her.

Remember, you can encourage your child; you can be supportive and create a climate for healing, but you cannot be the therapist. With proper help, your child will likely work through this season of depression and be able to move toward independence.

PASSIVE-AGGRESSIVE BEHAVIOR

Our nation has significant problems with anger. From road rage to verbal or physical abuse in homes, violence occurs on all levels of American life. Anger takes many forms and improperly handled can cause many issues,[4] but here we'll discuss how anger can be an underlying cause of passive-aggressive behavior. Like depression, it is a behavior that is not always identified, yet can trip up an adult.

A Definition

First, a simple definition for an often misunderstood term. Passive-aggressive behavior becomes a pattern of "indirectly expressing negative feelings instead of openly addressing them" in a healthy manner.[5] If someone makes a suggestion or a request, the passive-aggressive person will appear to agree. But then he or she will fail to comply, possibly due to anger or resentment. Typically, the behavior opposes what an authority figure wants done; the angry individual intends to upset or anger the authority figure.

Passive-aggressive behavior is the worst way to handle one's anger because it is a choice to do wrong and can become part of one's character. Although it begins as a subconscious choice, it can to some extent become conscious. If passive-aggressive behavior is not understood and dealt with, it can harm and even destroy a person's life. That's what almost happened to Joel, who lost three jobs and then returned home to live with his parents.

Joel was an outgoing, well-liked young man. Bright, good-looking, and talented in many areas, he took his first position with a manufacturing company immediately after college. He liked the job (it was related to his area of study), and he did very well at first. After six months, he received a good evaluation and a bonus. His parents were pleased for him.

However, a year later, Joel's attitude was changing. He began to be irritable when asked to do something requiring extra effort and started complaining to fellow employees about the company. When he missed meetings or came to work late, he made excuses. As the quality of his work diminished, the more important tasks were assigned to other employees. His boss did everything he could to help Joel, spending extra time with him to encourage him. He even changed his responsibilities, giving him work that he thought Joel would enjoy more. Nothing seemed to work, because Joel always found a way to fail.

When eventually he was fired, he complained bitterly that he had been wronged. He threatened to sue the company and called an attorney. As the two talked, the attorney told him that he had no basis for a suit, but Joel did not believe him.

Joel managed to be hired by another company, but he displayed the same kind of behavior, and within two years he was terminated there also. After a third such failure, Joel returned home to live with his parents.

They were bewildered but supported him in the best ways they knew and had a surprisingly good relationship with him. Eight months later, Joel was still living at home and making little effort to find another job. His parents, believing he was angry and depressed, convinced him to receive counseling.

The counselor concluded that Joel was indeed both clinically depressed and angry. Since she determined that his depression increased his anger, she knew the combination aggravated the acting out of his anger in passive-aggressive ways. The counselor treated the depression first. As he responded to treatment and his anger subsided, she was able to teach Joel how to manage anger maturely rather than resort to passive-aggressive behavior.

There's a happy ending to Joel's story. It took Joel and his counselor more than a year of working together to make good headway. He is now able to understand the underlying cause of his puzzling behavior and is continuing to make progress in controlling it. Passive-aggressive ways of handling anger are difficult to treat, but persistence will pay off. Therapy is usually the only approach to treating it.

Recognizing Passive-Aggressive Behavior

First, now that you have seen an example of this behavior, let's look at how to recognize it in those you know. Specific signs include:

Resentment and opposition to others' demands

Procrastination

Intentional mistakes

Noncooperative action (or inaction)

Sullen, even hostile attitude

Complaining

Declaring one is not appreciated[6]

For Joel, it made no sense for him to fail in the workplace. He had everything he needed to succeed—he was trained in the field and was initially competent. Even when he tried to do well, he subconsciously managed to act out against authority, without understanding his motivation in doing so.

Second, you can suspect passive-aggressive behavior when nothing you do to correct the behavior works. Remember, the purpose of passive-aggressive behavior is often to upset an authority figure or to generally just not be cooperative; therefore, your adult child will resist all your efforts as one in authority to change him or her.

Third, even though the purpose of much passive-aggressive behavior is to upset the authority figure, it is the passive-aggressive person who actually gets hurt and suffers the ongoing consequences. Joel's behavior was subconsciously designed to upset the employer, but it was Joel, not the employer, who suffered the consequences. Unless he changed his immature way of handling anger, Joel would continue to manifest it passive-aggressively with family members and future employers. He would likely have problems with spiritual authority also.

If your child is handling anger passive-aggressively to such an extent that it is hurting him, you will want to find a way for him to get the help he needs. Counseling is important, but timing is crucial. He must be at the point where he genuinely seeks ways to change his behavior.

If you are feeling his behavior is illogical, rebellious, and self-destructive, it may be he is displaying passive-aggressive anger. And you may need to act not only for your his welfare, but for your own.

SUBSTANCE ABUSE

Substance use, legal or illegal, is not a new occurrence in our culture. With the legalization of recreational marijuana in many states—and even before that—a concert-goer or someone attending an outdoor sporting event can expect to be exposed to the aroma of pot smoke and even experience a "contact high." Even more concerning, marijuana is more potent than it once was.[7] Statistics on overdoses and death from fentanyl and other opioids are grim. Party drugs and hallucinogens are in widespread use in some circles, and alcohol- and drug-related problems have become a national scandal.

But though studies are often conducted and a plethora of information is readily available, if your loved one has a substance use disorder, you don't want statistics. You want to help.

Misusing alcohol and drugs may connect with some of the factors we have talked about in this and other chapters, whether as a primary means of coping with the pressures of being a young adult or recreational substance use that has gotten out of hand.

Although alcohol is reported as being beneficial to health in limited quantities, we know that even a small amount of alcohol can cause radical changes in personality and behavior. In larger quantities, it can have harmful and even destructive effects, physically and psychologically.

Similarly, some prescription drugs and others sold over the counter are habituating. If your adult child has an ongoing prescription for a painkiller or sedative, watch him and be aware of the medication's addictive properties. If you believe your child is addicted to a prescription medication, contact his physician. When such drugs are taken with alcohol, they are even more dangerous and can lead to death. Both nonprescribed and prescribed drugs used not according to directions—that is, abused—will have harmful effects over the short- and long-term, as will the abuse of alcohol.

Some short-term effects are drowsiness, poor coordination, impairment of judgment, and decreased reflexes. Long-term effects can be permanent problems with memory, and damage to the liver, brain, vascular system, and central nervous system. There is little doubt that abuse has wreaked havoc among a segment of adult children who return (or stay) home as they support an addiction or lose a job because of an addiction. Often they are skilled at hiding their substance abuse.

You may dismiss this as a possible reason for your adult child to be at home, or you may believe your child is addicted and want him to leave your home. Let's recognize, though, there are reasons our children may fall into a substance addiction, and a compassionate but firm response is in order.

First, as the stress in our society increases, the use of drugs also increases. That's a key reason drug and alcohol abuse continues to thrive among our hurting young adults. Stress causes fear, anxiety, depression, tension, nervousness, and dysphasia (becoming unable to use or understand language). When these become unbearable, as they do in some people, drugs can induce pleasant-feeling states such as relaxation, calmness, euphoria, power, and invulnerability. As the pace of life grows more hectic, and as our society becomes more impersonal and alien, those most vulnerable will experience a loss of control over their own lives because of their extreme anxiety. In an intense and fast-paced social climate, chemicals present a very real temptation.

Responding to Substance Addiction

When parents realize that an adult child has a chemical problem, they are often the ones who will have to initiate some sort of intervention or suggest treatment. However, they are in a difficult position because their child may deny having a problem. A daughter may say she only drinks "on occasion" and can put the bottle or glass down whenever she wants to; she may envision an alcoholic as someone who is in a continual stupor, which she clearly is not. It is easy for someone to drink enough beer to qualify as an alcoholic but still assume that she is fine, because one glass of beer is relatively low in alcohol content. All persons who drink have their own idea of what is an appropriate amount to consume. However, most communities have information centers where you can find out what qualifies as alcoholism rather than social drinking. You can also find out about treatment possibilities and groups such as Celebrate Recovery, Alcoholics Anonymous, and Al-Anon and Alateen for family members.

> *This is the best advice I can give: seek counsel from a qualified person on what steps you should take.*

Drug users also can be creative in denying their problems. Your son may admit to using marijuana but say, "I'm not taking the hard stuff like cocaine, and I don't plan to." Or he may say it is only for recreational use, is relaxing, and won't lead to addiction. As noted, drugs can produce pleasant feelings of relaxation, calmness, and euphoria. But they also enslave, creating a dependence for false, temporary feelings of comfort. Further, "there is a lot of misinformation in the public sphere about cannabis and its effects on psychological health, with many assuming that this drug is safe to use with no side effects," cautions Dr. David Gorelick, a professor of psychiatry at the University of Maryland School of Medicine in Baltimore.[8] Use of marijuana is cited for 10 percent of drug-related emergency room visits.[9]

A chemical dependency problem is treated as an illness. Use language with your grown child that indicates they have a problem or illness, rather than he or she *is* the problem. Say "person with a substance/alcohol use disorder" rather than user, substance abuser, alcoholic, and so on. Even "habit" is not considered a helpful word since it implies a simple fix, as though the person can just choose to stop.[10] Sometimes dependency has gone beyond that.

This is the best advice I can give: seek counsel from a qualified person on what steps you should take. Handling such a situation yourself is extremely difficult and sensitive, and it is so easy to make a bad case even worse. You want to avoid being in the position of provoker or enabler.

Seek encouragement through prayer. Remember, God answers prayer. He can guide you to the best sources of help as well as to the best attitudes and actions that will benefit your child and your entire family. Wisely share your concerns with someone in your church, enlisting others to pray, or with trusted members of your community. You won't feel so alone.

It is hard, but sometimes you must allow your adult children to suffer the consequences of their drug and alcohol abuse. This is the fastest way for young persons to become willing to go for treatment. Parents need to be kind but firm in refusing to pick up the pieces when their child gets into trouble. Most persons with a substance use disorder are not open to treatment until they get to the end of their rope. This "nowhere else to turn" state of mind may come through loss of a job, health concerns, the fear of losing one's spouse, children, or another valued personal relationship.

Prevention

Better than treating for drug or alcohol abuse is preventing it. You have been and continue to be a model in your own attitudes toward drugs of all kinds. The best model for our children and also the surest protection from becoming addicted ourselves is to abstain from using alcohol or marijuana ourselves as parents. Sadly, more than 14 million adults in the United States have a drinking problem,[11] and about "178,000 people die from excessive alcohol use in the U.S. each year."[12] According to the National Highway Traffic Safety Administration, "every day, about 37 people in the United States die in drunk-driving crashes—that's one person every 39 minutes."[13] Fatalities involving cannabis use have also increased, and one reason is ignorance. A study showed that some people who ingested or inhaled marijuana believed they were ready to drive after ninety minutes, but their performance in a simulated vehicle was as poor as a half hour after using the drug.[14] (Statistics like these are often updated and will vary among sources, but the point is that substance abuse is a serious problem.) It is true that some young adults who grew up in homes where parents were abstainers became alcoholics and drug addicts, but their numbers are minuscule compared to those who grew up in homes where parents modeled only social drinking. We need a radical shift in our thinking and living if we are going to turn the tide against the devastating results of alcohol and drug abuse in our society.

If your child is addicted to drugs or alcohol, the only lasting solution is to get him or her into a treatment program.

The most effective way to keep your young adult child from getting involved in drugs and alcohol is to love them unconditionally, speaking love in a language that communicates to them emotionally, and keeping their love tanks full—while also modeling for them a life of abstinence from drugs and alcohol. In so doing, you can demonstrate to them both while they are still under your roof and more impressionable and later on that one can experience life to the fullest without reliance on external chemical influence. Many parents may disagree, but after many years in ministry and family counseling, I deeply believe abstinence is the best policy, sending a consistent signal to our children. Some of the benefits of abstaining are sleeping better, having more energy, weight loss, lower blood pressure, and even having more money.[15]

If your child is already using drugs and/or alcohol but is not at the point of having a substance use disorder, be sure you give unconditional love and also educational information about the dangers of consumption. If, however, your child is already addicted to drugs or alcohol, the only lasting solution is to get him or her into a treatment program. This means you will need to do your homework about the various kinds of programs as well as their cost.

ATTENTION-DEFICIT/HYPERACTIVITY DISORDER

Kathleen gathered everything she needed for the meeting and stuffed it all in her pack. Her phone was already on the side pocket from earlier in the day, and she had to remember to stop on the way to pick up a thank-you note for the others to sign.

In her late twenties, Kathleen lived with her divorced mother, an arrangement that suited both easygoing women. By taking the overnight shift at an assisted living facility, Kathleen had a chance to make a reasonable living, save money, and not have to interact much with people. It was a good enough job, though she made several mistakes from not bothering to read the company's guidelines. It was a long and boring manual, and she figured she'd do better by learning on the job.

At her mother's prodding, she had recently decided to develop outside interests. She joined a gym and sometimes stopped on her way home from work early in the morning. She signed up for a discussion group that met two evenings a month at the library, and even volunteered to coordinate small groups at her church.

Unfortunately, her attendance at the gym was spotty. She often forgot to bring a combination lock and was uncomfortable leaving her belongings in an open locker while she worked out. On those days, she just went home. Twice she had read the wrong material for the discussion group, which didn't stop her from interrupting others who were offering their opinions on the story or essay. She sensed that people were starting to react to her with impatience, but that was their problem.

People at the church were friendly and, as often happens, were happy to have a new person for a committee, where being available and willing were the most important qualifications. They loaded Kathleen with tasks. Her role would be to keep records of who was in what group, what they were studying, when they met, and what kind of results and feedback they were getting. Tonight she was on her way to her second meeting with the Study Buddies, who oversaw the groups.

After the greetings, Kathleen was asked for the thank-you card she had promised to bring. The Buddies were to sign a card of appreciation for a member who had served for several years and was now cycling out. Kathleen rummaged through her bag, but it was nowhere to be found. Then she remembered she had forgotten to purchase one. She said she'd phone her mother, who could easily pick up a card and bring it to the church, but her phone wasn't in the side pocket after all. When it came time for her to present her report on members in each small group, she found she had neglected to include some vital information, such as leaders' names and when the various groups met. She remembered then that someone had given her a list of her duties clearly spelled out, but it was printed on a font she didn't like, and she put off looking at it. The meeting was starting to drag, so she left the circle to find the coffee.

If you suspect that your adult child is afflicted with ADHD, I encourage you to read books and articles by reputable professionals in the field. There is much controversy surrounding ADHD and much erroneous material is being written. Your healthcare professional should be able to guide you to trustworthy information. In addition, your local medical society is a good source of beginning to find the best help in your area.

ADHD is a "neuro-developmental disorder charactered by difficulty sustaining attention," or a combination of this difficulty plus hyperactive or impulsive behaviors.[16] This condition is most often diagnosed in childhood and can last into adulthood. Some of the symptoms that exhibit in adults with ADHD are unfinished tasks, forgetfulness, losing things, carelessness, recklessness, poor organizational skills, interrupting.[17] If your adult child exhibits these behaviors, his success as an independent adult will be delayed. Just from reading this limited list of indicators of ADHD, you may recognize why your child has difficulty at school or work, with relationships, and with typical tasks of daily life.

The treatment of ADHD in adults, as well as children, must be tailored to the individual because each person responds differently. Professional counseling will help with organizational skills, reducing impulsive behavior, a plan for controlling his temper, and so on. The Mayo Clinic reports that treatments for ADHD "typically involve medication, education, skills training, and psychological counseling. A combination of these is often the most effective treatment."[18] As the parent, you can suggest helpful strategies such as using sticky notes or an electronic device for keeping track of things he'll need to remember; break tasks into steps so nothing feels too overwhelming to accomplish; set up a file system to organize information and stay with it; keep items such as keys or phone in the same place. And let your adult child know to ask for help!

The serious issues that have been covered in this chapter show that sometimes there are concerns that require more help that even the most well-meaning parent can give. When it is time to consult a professional and encourage your adult child to do so, know you are on the right path to secure change and a hopeful future for your son or daughter.

Adapting to Your Changing Role

six

Caring for Yourself

Serena saw on the ID that her niece Jackie was calling.

"Yeee-sss?" she said in the genie voice that was a habit between the two.

"Aunt Serena, guess what? I'm pregnant! Don and I are having a baby!"

"Oh, that's wonderful!" Serena told her. She added sincerely, "You two are in for some of the very best times of your life!" What Serena thought but did not voice was, *You're likely also in for more heartache than you can ever imagine.*

Someone has said that when children are little, they step all over your feet, and when they are older, they step all over your heart. The rigors of raising children can be extremely draining, physically, emotionally, and financially. By the time children reach young adulthood, many parents feel depleted. Parenting can be hazardous to your health.

"I thought that by this time we would be living on easy street, enjoying the fruit of our labors," one father said. "Instead, we have spent much of our retirement funds on lawyers, trying to help our son with his complicated legal matters. Now we've even sold our house and moved to a smaller place to reduce our monthly bills. If anything else happens, I don't know what we'll do. We're at the end of our rope."

Wendy's daughter married a man who was underemployed—working, but not making enough to provide well for their family of five. Wendy, who was divorced and had supported herself for many years, helped often and was starting to resent it. She didn't want her three grandchildren to be deprived due to their parents' shortcomings, but her own piggy bank had its limitations, and she had planned on doing some traveling at this stage of her own life.

Another couple had a son-in-law who often traveled for work, and their daughter was uncomfortable being alone with a toddler and newborn. So the couple frequently spent several days at a time in their daughter's home helping with the young ones and were glad to help—but had begun to confide in each other that they would like to be home among their own things and following their own routine more often.

When real emergencies or unavoidable problems assail their grown children, many parents feel bound to help. Sometimes the situation is not even due to ill-advised behavior: the child has an illness or disability, or things just happen in life. Whatever the problem or its cause, the long-term toll on parents can be significant. Though the parents do care about the struggles of their children, they may have little strength, emotional energy, or money to make a difference. Often the parents find their own reserve tanks are empty.

MANAGE YOUR RESOURCES

We parents, who naturally love our children, want to help. But how much can we do? How much should we do? Like the pink Energizer bunny who keeps going and going and going—and as a marketing tool has been going for decades—we may keep giving and giving and giving. But unlike the rabbit, we may soon find our energy reserves drained. Wise parents recognize that physical, emotional, and financial resources always have limits.

The most common problem in parenting your adult child is overreacting to a crisis in the child's life. Parents may spend many resources trying to help the child through the crisis, only to find six months later that they are embroiled in yet another crisis. It is important that parents manage their physical and material resources prudently, so that they can be available to their children when there is real need.

Heidi and Kurt wish that someone had helped them understand this reality earlier in their relationship with their son, Brent. Unknown to them, he developed an alcohol addiction during his college years, but still finished his studies and earned a degree. When he entered the workforce, Brent was overwhelmed by the stresses of corporate life and sought relief in alcohol. He told himself and others, "I just need something to help me unwind at night." He wouldn't admit that he had a problem.

In his first two years of work, Brent had three different jobs, always quitting just before he was about to be fired. Between jobs, his parents supported him by paying his rent and giving him a living allowance. Each time Brent would sober up long enough to find a new job, but within a year he was unemployed again.

When he quit his third job, his parents forced him into an expensive treatment center, for which they paid. Two weeks after he was released, he was drunk. This time his parents were so exasperated that they wrote him off, telling him that he was no longer welcome in their home until he got his life straightened out. The stress had been just too much for Heidi and Kurt. Both had medical problems of their own, and Heidi was also caring for her aging parents. They were emotionally depleted.

The story might have been different had they asked, as soon as they knew Brent had a problem, "What is the best way to help him?" This might have led them to admit their lack of knowledge about alcoholism and their need for outside help. Kurt and Heidi might have attended an Al-Anon meeting for family members of alcoholics, where they would have found good information and a supportive group. They would likely have made wiser decisions, conserved their financial resources until Brent was ready to benefit from a treatment program, and learned positive steps toward preserving their physical and emotional health.

Too many parents make the mistake of trying to deal with the crises of their adult children without reaching out to others who have gone through similar experiences. When they do not seek available help, parents often lose themselves while trying to save their children. Many an older couple has ended up divorcing after having expended all their energies trying to help their adult children and failing to nurture their own relationship.

GIVE YOUR CHILD FREEDOM TO MATURE

Remember that your young adult child must live his own life, and that means solving his own problems. If you step in, you short-circuit the process of your child's emerging maturity. Your caring role is to give love, acceptance, encouragement, and guidance when requested. Many parents find this more difficult than stepping in to solve the problem.

As has been suggested in other chapters, it is crucial that you set boundaries for what is and is not acceptable behavior in the family setting. Once these boundaries are established, family members can hold one another accountable to staying within them. That often means allowing a child the freedom to take whatever course of action seems appropriate, even in a time of crisis. That there is an emergency does not negate the fact that the child is an adult.

Parents whose children are going through crises must maintain the balance between self-preservation and self-sacrifice. That, of course, can be a major challenge. On the one hand, we want to help them, for the noblest of all callings is the one to serve. And we can serve those we love—but always within limits. On the other hand, we must maintain our own health. Interestingly, Jesus of Nazareth, recognized by Christians and many non-Christians as the world's greatest example of a loving leader,

A comic strip mom told her son that his bags for college were packed and by the door. "I washed and folded your laundry, I mended your backpack . . . I fixed the zipper on your jacket, and put a cheque in the pocket." The dad asked if she'd gotten his bus ticket. "Of course not," she retorted. "How is he going to survive in this world if we do everything for him?"[1]

once said He "did not come to be served, but to serve."[2] His life was characterized by self-sacrifice for the benefit of others. However, those who recorded His life indicated that at various times Jesus chose to withdraw from the crowds and retreat to a secluded spot for rest and prayer.[3] Restoring His own physical and spiritual strength was important to Him; so it should be for us.

GUARD YOUR WELL-BEING

Your body requires proper maintenance. Without nutritious food, moderate exercise, and adequate sleep, your body can succumb to illness, disease, and possibly premature death. Do not allow your children's problems to keep you from the essentials for staying physically healthy.

The same is true of emotional health—you cannot ignore your own emotional needs and still expect to give continued help to your children over the long haul. For example, your own need for love requires that you spend time enriching your marriage and/or your relationship with family and friends. Your need for order or structure means that you will set boundaries both on yourself and your children. Your need for recreation and relaxation is fully as important as your desire to help your children.

Becoming emotionally obsessed with the problems of adult children can bring one to a point of emotional exhaustion where they are no longer able to help at all.

One mother who realized this truth once told us: "I do water aerobics three times a week. If I didn't, I couldn't continue to help my son and his wife as they cope with the trauma of his cancer."

Attending concerts and community theater productions, doing physical exercise, gardening, fishing, playing golf, and scores of other activities divert the mind, emotions, and body from otherwise overwhelming stresses.

Some parents feel guilty enjoying themselves when their children are in painful crises. However, becoming emotionally obsessed with the problems of adult children can bring one to a point of emotional exhaustion where they are no longer able to help at all. Therefore, regard your times of recreation as essential to your emotional health, as essential as food is to your physical health.

> Life is a gift and a challenge.
> — Jay Payleitner

Also maintain your spiritual health. Your spiritual nature is often expressed in your desire for significance. Deep within all of us is a motivation to live in such a way as to make an impact on generations to come and to invest in things that count beyond the grave. Materialism is not an adequate base to satisfy these yearnings for ultimate significance. It is those yearnings for significance—inherently a spiritual quest—that motivates our noblest efforts at doing good in the world.

Most people know that the idea of significance is meaningless if there is not some ultimate authority that determines what is noble or ignoble, what is truly significant. For those in the Jewish and Christian traditions, the road to ultimate authority has led to the God of the Old and New Testaments, who, from the dawn of humankind's creation, has reached out to relate to His creatures. They believe that God revealed His moral law in the Bible. Those in the Christian tradition also believe God has sent as the Messiah Jesus, who demonstrated what significant living is all about and how it may be obtained. In both traditions, Jews and Christians agree that taking time to establish and maintain our relationship with God is vital to maintaining spiritual health.

Having personal, regular times with God through praying, reading Scripture, and meditating on it are exercises that feed the soul. This daily time with God can become a healthy way of life, as important to our spiritual nature as food, exercise, and sleep are to the body.

For many who did not grow up in a religious tradition, a crisis in the life of one of their adult children or in their own lives often will awaken the reality of their need for spiritual help. For example, alcohol and drug addiction has led thousands of people to acknowledge two of the Twelve Steps of the Alcoholics Anonymous program: that they need supernatural power and to turn their lives over to "the care of God" as they understand Him.[4] Such a discovery has been the beginning of a whole new dimension of life for these adults. They are not ashamed of the spiritual comfort they receive. Instead, they have acknowledged their need for God and found it a welcome first step in filling the spiritual void with which they have lived. For those who are looking for a more overtly biblical approach "to find community and freedom from the issues that are controlling" their lives, Celebrate Recovery is available for "anyone struggling with hurts, hang-ups, and habits of any kind."[5]

It is easy to agree that self-care is important and not to be neglected; it is another to proactively ensure that you follow through. See if you can take one step for yourself today—whether it's physical through exercise and better nutrition; intellectual through learning or trying something new; emotional by getting a handle on worrying and determining to feel happier; or spiritual by pursuing greater peace. Not only will you benefit, but your adult children will too.

seven

Lifestyle Issues

There he was sipping coffee at a table at the back of the shop. Since when had Les Harper become a consumer of gourmet coffee? Megan wouldn't have thought he was the type.

She knew Les from church. She didn't know him well, but she and the retired teacher often said hello when they crossed paths, and it was always a pleasant exchange. "How are you doing, Megan?" he would ask. And invariably her response followed the outline: "Fine. Good. You?" and then a few minutes of friendly chat would take place. Today he saw her and waved and, though she had intended to grab her own drink and leave, she didn't want to appear unfriendly. She made her way to his table, smiled, and prepared for the routine.

"How are you doing, Megan?" Les asked.

"Fine. Good. You?"

He didn't follow the script but paused. Then said, "Now, Megan, you say fine but I don't think you are. You look like something's on your mind."

Megan was appalled, though she kept the smile pasted on. Les was a respected leader in the church, active in the community, reliable.

A pillar. His family was perfect. Though she didn't know them, his three grown children were certainly successful, productive citizens, married to amazing spouses. What was she supposed to say to this man? Suddenly, she blurted it out.

"My daughter's been living with her boyfriend," she heard herself say. "I feel like she's going the wrong way in life."

"Oh, Megan," perfect-family Les said. "My daughter was in the same situation." And he proceeded to tell Megan the story.

"My" Truth or Truth?

For many people, what some of us think of as traditional values— or basically shared societal mores and norms—have been replaced by an attitude of "whatever's right for me is right. It's none of my business how you live and not your business how I live." The assumption is that right and wrong are relative. Morality? There are no moral absolutes. We no longer talk about truth, but "my truth," meaning we each have our own experiences, so there can be many perspectives of what truth actually is. If you and your adult child have different values, you may chafe at the lifestyle they practice or advocate, especially if he or she is living at home.

Whether you continue to believe in moral absolutes or simply prefer that your children not engage in behavior that makes you uncomfortable, you probably are disturbed when you watch your children follow a morally ambiguous road. When they visit or live in their parents' homes—or when you visit them in theirs—conflict over lifestyle choices is often present, almost inevitable. As a parent, you may feel intense emotional pain, disrespect, or even rejection when the choices of your adult children violate your standards of behavior and beliefs.

Too often we're reluctant to share our real lives with others, fearing their judgment or condemnation. This tendency is compounded when it comes to our adult children, as we don't necessarily want to share their situations with our friends, and part of that is not wanting others to think ill of them.

But it's a reality that often adult children are living lifestyles and making choices that are contrary to the way they were raised. Sometimes their lifestyles raise serious issues with your own values. Other times their choices are just preferences.

In this chapter, we'll talk about some of these issues: cohabitation, homosexuality, gender issues, religious choices, gaming, and money. And how you can love your adult children when their lifestyle isn't pleasing to you, and you believe it's harmful to them.

COHABITATION

In the anecdote above, Megan was upset about her daughter living with her boyfriend. Not only did it go against her own values, but common sense told her it wasn't a wise choice to make, nor did it bode well for a stable future. And she didn't especially want her friends to know.

When Megan's daughter Debi met Hudson, the two quickly hit it off and moved in together. The couple hasn't ruled out marriage. They just don't feel it's time or necessary. Everything is going well without it. And as Debi has pointed out, no one cares about marriage anymore. It's not as important "as when you were young, Mom." And Megan likes Hudson. She just can't understand the in-between concept of not moving ahead in a relationship to the next logical step: marriage.

While living together before or instead of marriage was once uncommon in the US, both statistics and what we observe just by looking around indicate that this is no longer the case. In addition, many people—about 65 percent—believe that a marriage has more chance of success if a couple lives together first.[1] However, "there is *no evidence* that this is generally true and *a lot of evidence* that it is not true."[2]

Cohabiting means living in the same dwelling in order to enjoy the pleasures of marriage, especially sexual relations, without the responsibility of marriage.

Cohabitation is fast becoming an acceptable lifestyle for couples of all ages. Now unmarried men and women live in the same house for months, even years, before getting married—if they marry at all. About half of all children born in the US are now born to unmarried couples. Many young people believe living together without benefit of marriage is a totally justified way of forming life's most intimate relationship. Permissive influences in society and fear of commitment are the main reasons they cohabit, and they find their choice glorified in the media and taken for granted by many of their peers, so they share meals, money, and bed.

One study asked couples why they chose living together over marriage, and gave four possible responses: for financial reasons, to test the relationship, to spend more time together, and for convenience.[3] "Identifying the reason why you want to move in together is just as important as identifying the reason why you want to get married," professor Galena Rhoades points out.[4] Spending more time together was the most common of the four choices given in the study. The researchers concluded that many couples "slide" into living together more than making a solid decision to do so with a plan.

In Debi and Hudson's case, they decided they wanted to spend more time together, and financially it made sense to share an apartment. So, what are parents to do when they find themselves in conflict with their child's sexual behavior? How should Megan and her husband, Max, respond?

Keep Communicating

Some parents have tried the ostrich approach, denying what is happening. There is little to be gained from this approach except perhaps momentary peace of mind. Sooner or later, reality will be unavoidable. Other parents use the missile approach—taking every opportunity to shoot verbal zingers at the young people to condemn their behavior. Such reaction damages parental influence now and in the future.

Our attitudes as parents are important. If we are upset, belligerent, or scold our children who have live-in arrangements, they will likely display an even more tenacious defiance. It is usually better for parents to express their beliefs in tones as gentle as possible and then leave it. Parents need to remember that the only chance they have for influencing their children is through the relationship that already exists between the parent and the adult child.

It is usually best to treat your child's live-in mate as a likable person and show common courtesies to him or her.

So Max and Megan decided to keep communication open. Debi's world no longer revolved around her parents and family home, as is expected when a child becomes an adult, but her relationship with Hudson was primary. Megan missed the closeness she had once had with Debi, but recognized she had to accept the new situation.

She was also wise enough to know that unwarranted criticism of Hudson would turn Debi away from her and toward Hudson. And Megan did like Hudson—he had a responsible job and was good to Debi. Debi's dad, Max, didn't have much respect for Hudson.

> A great marriage is not when the "perfect couple" comes together. It is when an imperfect couple learns to enjoy their differences.
>
> — Dave Meurer

To Max, a man behaves like an adult and makes a commitment to be a husband, not just a boyfriend. But he agreed with Megan that no good would come of becoming estranged from the couple now if they wanted to continue a healthy relationship for the future—a future he hoped would include marriage.

It can be difficult for parents caught in this situation to be civil to a child's partner, and yet to be unpleasant is a serious mistake that can drive the child into a deeper commitment. Also, if your child ends up marrying the person, your future relationship with the young family is damaged. It is usually better to treat your child's live-in mate as a likable person and show common courtesies to him or her.

This may be extremely difficult for you, but with God's grace you can behave with love and kindness, even though you do not approve of their behavior. Your tone of voice, a handshake greeting, and occasional hugs all can help maintain an amicable relationship with the child and his or her friend. At the same time, you may caution and ask questions of your child about the relationship to show your concern and dissatisfaction with the live-in situation.

It is important that you have the support of family and friends;

you may even need counseling to be able to maintain an even attitude and behavior toward the young people. Also, you should remind yourself that your child loves you and needs you, and that he knows exactly how you are affected by his behavior. He knows that your continuing to be a loving parent does not mean that you approve of what he is doing or that you are violating your own values.

Just as you have sought to give your child unconditional love in the past, regardless of behavior, so also you will do the same now. You want to be a positive influence on your child in the future, and this means that you cannot afford to break the relationship you have.

Open Dialogue

Many young adults have jettisoned the concept of parental authority. Their attitude seems to be, "Why should we listen to you?" If we are to have a positive influence on them, whether it be about a cohabitation arrangement or other lifestyle choices, we must seek to relate to them as persons. That includes being willing to listen to their ideas, consider their points of view, and affirm their logic and perspectives where we can. Honestly disagree where you must; ask probing questions without feeling that you need to answer your own questions. Expose your children to the results of modern social research on the consequences of certain sexual lifestyles but let them wrestle with the realities of the research;[5] and don't preach.

This does not mean that you should not share your distress at what you believe to be wrong choices: it does mean that you will not use that distress as a tool of manipulation. You can offer non-condemning statements that you hope will create a climate where the young adults can receive and even request your advice. It is crucial that you recognize their autonomy and give them freedom to make their own choices, even when you disagree with them.

They may well suffer the consequences of those choices, and you can certainly walk with them through those painful consequences. That's part of being redemptive. It is in this context that many parents build deep and abiding relationships with their broken and suffering young adults. Your emotional support may be what they need to help them make corrections in this part of life.

Max and Megan

Max and Megan welcomed Hudson to family gatherings such as birthdays or barbecues. But they had a hard time sharing the couple with Hudson's family for other occasions, especially holidays. The first Thanksgiving Debi spent with Hudson's family was difficult for Megan and Max. When his mother invited them to a holiday party before Christmas that year, they accepted, wanting to be friendly to these new people in their daughter's life.

It turned out that Hudson's parents had divorced some years before, so they were meeting his mother and stepfather. Hudson and his stepfather were cordial, but not close. As Max and Megan met more people at the party and navigated some of the complex relationships, they began to understand better Hudson's reluctance to commit to marriage. And no one they encountered expressed any qualms about Hudson and Debi's living situation—they all "just loved Debi" and said she was perfect for Hudson. Max and Megan were rather dispirited by the time the evening ended and they were on their way home.

Hudson and Debi continued living together for three more years with no plans for marriage, at least not that they shared with Debi's parents. So Max and Megan decided that being pleasant, keeping communication open, and continuing to show love were all ways they could respond to their daughter's cohabitation situation, though it was a persistent source of grief to them. They made an intentional decision that maintaining a relationship with Debi and Hudson was critical. And over time, as they got to know Hudson well, they realized that he was actually a good match for Debi, though they still hoped they would get married. Because Max and Megan had a deep Christian faith, they continued to pray fervently about the situation and asked friends to pray with them.

One evening, Hudson and Debi invited Max and Megan to their apartment for dessert and actually asked their advice about planning for marriage. They said they were ready to take their relationship to the next "best step," as Hudson put it. Debi told her parents that their kindness to the couple over the years had greatly influenced their decision to "make it work" and that she appreciated they had welcomed and shown love to Hudson. Max and Megan were thrilled when the couple announced they had set a wedding date—a simple ceremony and soon. They were further pleased when they agreed to meet up with their pastor to ask him to conduct their nuptials.

Max and Megan drove home that evening thankful that their prayers were being answered and profoundly grateful that as parents they hadn't said or done anything that would have alienated their daughter.

If you have a situation similar to this one and you have handled it well, but it has not turned out as satisfactorily, don't despair. Don't second-guess yourself and wonder if you should have been more forceful, confronting, demanding. Or, if you have been inappropriately overbearing, demanding, or otherwise unpleasant, you can always apologize and start on a better road with your loved one. And prayer can prepare your heart, giving you sensitivity, wisdom, and peace.[6]

HOMOSEXUALITY

It is no longer newsworthy for anyone in public life to identify as a homosexual. Television programs and commercials depict gay people and same-sex couples as ordinary. School bulletin boards are decorated with "open hearts" art, and store displays prominently feature pride-themed accessories.

Early in the twenty-first century, 60 percent of Americans opposed same-sex marriage, according to a poll by Pew Research. Fifteen years later 61 percent supported it.[7] Same-sex couples apply to become foster and adoptive parents, and agencies that will only place children with heterosexuals may find their government funding at risk. With the *Obergefell v. Hodges* decision in 2015, same-sex marriage was legalized in all fifty states. "You can't find another issue where attitudes have shifted so rapidly," observed political science professor Don Haider-Markel.[8]

Despite the changing cultural mores on the issues surrounding homosexuality, almost all parents—even those who say they will tolerate many lifestyles—will feel shock and deep hurt if one of their children announces they are gay. Though some parents may have suspected that their child had homosexual tendencies, most parents assume their children are heterosexual; they will be devastated if their children reveal a strong sexual attraction for the same sex. An initial reaction is that they as parents must have failed their child in some crucial way. For this reason, many adult children don't readily or ever announce their same-sex attraction or involvement in this lifestyle.

But for our purposes here, let's assume your child has been forthcoming. As a parent, be aware that in most cases if one has a strong homosexual desire, the attraction to members of the same sex will continue even if the individual chooses a heterosexual or celibate lifestyle. Because this is so, parents must deal with the situation and come to some resolution.

Distinguish Orientation from Lifestyle

Significantly, parents must distinguish between a homosexual orientation and a homosexual lifestyle. Orientation has to do with inner emotional and sexual desires, whereas lifestyle has to do with overt sexual behavior. Though a son or daughter is attracted to members of the same sex, he or she is not compelled to live a homosexual lifestyle. The person can show self-control and abstinence, even as an unmarried heterosexual can.

Same-sex attraction (SSA) is a complex topic, especially for religious parents. In the Judeo-Christian tradition, as in other major world religions, the homosexual lifestyle is viewed as abnormal and sinful, a departure from divinely ordained purposes of human sexuality.

A secular viewpoint is that same-sex attraction is morally neutral; it is not sinful, it is not desirable above another orientation, it's just the reality for some people. For those who believe SSA is voluntary, counselor Gene Burrus stresses that often "men and women who describe themselves as 'same-sex attracted' communicate their experience with a unique form of brokenness and suffering." He advises that religious people who sincerely believe same-sex attraction is sinful "listen to the specific challenges the same-sex attracted face."[9] As a parent, reflect on the courage it took for your child to share with you such a personal matter. Keep communication open: "How long have you felt this way? When did you decide you were attracted to the same sex?"

Doug says, "When I was in my late teens, I confessed to my home church that I was having same-sex attraction, though that's not what it was called back then. Two elders and the pastor took me aside and asked me not to return. This was over forty years ago. I have lived a celibate and happy life, but I couldn't describe myself as straight, if anyone asked. I'm thankful that young people who open up about their struggles are shown more Christian love these days."

No one has proved a genetic cause of homosexuality or that is an inherent, biological urge, so parents may be at a loss to understand why their child is same-sex attracted. No one knows why one child from a household turns out to be homosexual while the others are heterosexual. The young person goes through deep turmoil when she realizes that she is different from the norm, and this awareness may have begun in childhood or the teenage years. If she is part of a religious family, her pain can seem unbearable, since she knows that her orientation is condemned in the tradition in which she was raised.

You should also, as best you can, not worry about the responses of others, especially those of your religious tradition. What they may think is not as important as you loving your child. However, you might be surprised at the loving response of those in your religious community.

It may help religious parents empathize if they can realize that whether or not the homosexual child could or wants to change, she is still a person, their own child, created by God with inherent value and needing support as she finds her identity.

There continues to be much controversy, even among experts, on whether or not same-sex attraction is an aberration that can be treated. But regardless of how parents categorize homosexuality, it is present in a certain number of persons and needs to be dealt with in a redemptive manner. Here are some suggestions that may be helpful to you.

Accept Your Child

All parents who are having difficulty relating to their adult children who have revealed their same-sex attraction or who have even chosen a homosexual lifestyle should remember the central message of the Christian faith. The Scriptures declare loudly that "*all* have sinned."[10] We are not in a position to condemn our children for what we believe to be wrong or sinful behavior. Remember the words of Jesus when the crowds were ready to stone the woman who was caught in the act of adultery: "Let any one of you who is without sin be the first to throw a stone at her."[11] The Christian message is that we all are sinners equally fallen before a holy God who reached out to us by sending Christ to deliver us from sins.[12] Thus, we are to love all who stray, including our children, just as God loves us. Jesus was criticized by the religious people of His day because He associated with sinners, but He knew that He could not influence people without being with them.

As long as you are loving, kind, and as helpful as you can reasonably be, you are on the right track to gradually finding ways of having a more positive influence on the one you have raised.

We too will have our greatest influence if we accept our children, spend time with them, communicate with them, and demonstrate our love for them, even though we do not approve of their lifestyle.

Parents need to look beyond sexual orientation and love their son or daughter as a person. If we do not, we estrange them in our homes and our hearts. A Christian approach to gay persons or lesbians will be redemptive, not condemning. As Jill Savage explains, "One of the most important actions of truth is letting our kids know that no matter what, they're a part of your family. No matter what, you love them. No matter what, they are accepted. It's important to understand that acceptance doesn't mean agreeing with. It means accepting the reality of their circumstances. You may not agree with them and their choices, but no matter what, they will always be part of your family."[13]

You certainly have nothing to gain by rejecting your adult child if he or she is a practicing homosexual. You have much to gain if you continue to respect, love, and demonstrate that love to your child. This does not mean accepting a gay or lesbian lifestyle, nor does it mean enduring behavior that puts undue stress on you.

As long as you are loving, kind, and as helpful as you can reasonably be, you are on the right track to gradually finding ways of having a more positive influence on the one you have raised. As time passes, your own feelings will be more stable, as will your relationship with your child. Parents who reject their children, however, create unbelievable pain and often a permanent separation.

Some Practical Matters

If you have a warm relationship with your adult child and he has a relationship with another same-sex attracted person, you will probably be invited to be introduced to this friend. Some religious parents have chosen to not associate in any way with their adult child's romantic interest—which is their prerogative—but this may not be the best way, or the way you'll want to move forward. Should you welcome the friend to a family dinner? To a holiday celebration?

There is no set-in-stone response for every family or every circumstance. Family dynamics are complicated. If your son or daughter has newly come out to you as same-sex attracted, you might not be ready to meet a partner when a special occasion or holiday rolls around. If this is the case, you might just wisely and kindly say so. This isn't shutting the door to a later meeting or even socializing together, just giving yourself time to adjust.

> "Where too many Christian families go wrong is believing that they can't have a relationship with a child they disagree with or a child they feel is living a life outside of God's ways."[14]

On the other hand, you may be ready to meet your child's friend. It's up to you. Welcoming a guest to your home isn't the same as affirming what you believe to be a sinful lifestyle.

As parents, you have the right to maintain the rules of your home, which may include not having a friend share a bedroom with an unmarried partner. You may establish and enforce this principle with both a heterosexual and homosexual situation.

How you respond to your adult child's friend will also depend on whether you have younger siblings living in your home. "I don't feel okay with you and your partner showing physical affection in front of the younger children"[15] is an appropriate guideline for you to express. Such a reaction is not unloving to your gay child, but simply letting your conscience be your guide.

Find Help for Yourself

When you learn that your child is same-sex attracted, it is natural to grieve and to be concerned about his or her future. Again, it will be helpful to look beyond this development and see the person. Joe Dallas suggests, "Ask yourself this: Does the fact that he's gay, or that she's lesbian, cancel out all the other facts I know about him or her? Am I really not able to see and enjoy the wonderful person I've seen and enjoyed for so many years?"[16]

In whatever way you're dealing with this situation, you should seek help and support, and your particular circumstance will indicate the type of help you need. Therapy is often helpful to parents who are dealing with their responses to discovering they have a homosexual child, including feelings of confusion, depression, shock, and anxiety. Talking with a competent counselor can help you sort out those feelings, regain perspective, and learn how best to deal with the situation.

Support groups are particularly beneficial to parents of lesbian and gay children. As parents express their attitudes during the meetings, those attitudes and feelings can be dealt with in healthy and compassionate ways. Parents will discover that other fine people are experiencing the same pain, and they can share their ways of coping with the problems.

GENDER ISSUES

The evolving topic of gender issues can provoke rage, acceptance, denial, grief, fear, and other complicated emotions. From competition in sports to use of public bathrooms to using one's preferred pronoun to gender-neutral names and toys, the matter of gender can be a confusing topic to navigate.

Understanding the Terms

What is gender? Is it different than sex? Language changes in culture, and now gender means something different than simply male or female. "Gender" differs from sex in that gender accounts for identity and expression, referring to socially and culturally constructed behaviors and roles. In some circles, gender is fluid; that is, a person does not identify as having a fixed gender identity and may express themselves as masculine, feminine, or neutral at various times.

In psychology, *dysphoria* is "a mental state in which a person has a profound sense of unease or dissatisfaction."[17] Gender dysphoria refers to the feeling that a person's identity does not match the biological sex he or she was assigned at birth. Early onset gender dysphoria appears in childhood. Examples are a boy preferring to be around girls and doing "girlish" activities, or a girl doing "boyish" things. Some of these children will discard the behavior as they grow up, while others seek to live as a member of the opposite sex in adulthood.

Bear in mind that this is not about you or your parenting. It is also not a threat to your reputation. Thank your child for sharing with you and affirm your unconditional love.

Rapid onset gender dysphoria, ROGD, refers to the phenomenon presenting especially in early adolescence of those who previously showed no signs of identifying in any other way than their biological sex but who suddenly have decided they want to explore a change of genders. While ROGD is not a clinical term, it is real, and documented.[18] Some cite factors in ROGD such as social media influencers saluting gender fluidity, peers embracing transgender behavior as trendy, or clubs in schools promoting the acceptance of alternate lifestyles.[19]

It Takes Time to Process

For religious families especially, the discovery or affirmation that one's child or grandchild is experiencing gender dysphoria or even identifying as transgender can be very difficult to deal with. "Nope," one mother declared. "God made two sexes: male and female. Period. End of discussion." This woman sincerely believes that God made male and female as recounted in the biblical book of Genesis, and any deviation is based on false premises and sin. Yet, "end of discussion" is not a good way to express love and foster communication. Instead, if your loved one has revealed this information, you'll need to remember that, as an adult, he or she is old enough to work through these feelings and thoughts independently. You also have the right to need time to work through your own thoughts and feelings. "You've been thinking about this for a long time. Give me (or us) some time to process all this." Bear in mind that this is not about you or your parenting. It is also not a threat to your reputation. Thank your child for sharing with you and affirm your unconditional love. Your relationship is more than life circumstances.

When It's Your Family

"I am sad and grieve for the loss of my granddaughter," Susan began, speaking with her grief-sharing group. "It is not a typical kind of loss, but a loss all the same."

Susan told of how, at around four years old, her granddaughter showed a strong preference for boyish things: hairstyle, clothing, toys. Because there was a new baby boy in the family, it was thought that Danielle's behavior was a phase. But despite sessions with a child counselor, her preferences became more adamant and persistent.

"Middle school and puberty were challenging," Susan continued. "Trying to make her be more feminine led to mental and emotional distress, and we found out later that she had considered suicide. Fast-forward to now. Three years ago, she changed her name, and we were asked to use male pronouns. She is even taking hormones and has told us she will undergo sex change surgery."

For Susan this is very painful. But Danielle's parents seem accepting and comfortable with the situation, Susan explains. She adds that she has stressed that her love for the whole family and God's love for them will never change but admits it's just tough to talk about. The situation is compounded in that it's Susan's granddaughter who is transitioning, so she feels a generation removed for how far to go in conveying her own beliefs. She says, "It's a sensitive issue between my daughter and me. I am corrected if I don't use male pronouns."

Susan expressed appreciation for the grief-sharing group and for the support she has received from the close friends she has chosen to confide in. She appreciates the understanding feedback she has received from her support group and would encourage other parents and grandparents to share their struggles. "My hope is that my being open might help others going through this season."

If your adult child—or grandchild—is experiencing gender dysphoria or transgenderism, I encourage you, for your own mental and emotional health, to get counseling. You'll want to be in the best possible position to respond to this development in your loved one's life.

RELIGIOUS CHOICES

Another area in which young adults can provoke frustration in their parents is religion. Because religious beliefs are often tied strongly to our emotions or to family traditions, when adult children make religious choices that differ from those of their parents, we can feel great pain.

Our children's changing religious beliefs can express themselves in many ways. Besides choosing a different tradition, adult children may choose not to attend religious services at all. They may marry someone of a different faith or decide not to send their own children to church, feeling that "the children should be free to choose when they're older." These adult children may even join religious groups that the parents consider to be cultic and dangerous. Such decisions can make parents feel like failures. The decisions can also spark fear that the children are making a mistake that will have lasting consequences.

In addition, all religions include not only a core set of beliefs by which people try to live but numerous traditions that affect all of life. Our religious beliefs influence how we conduct weddings and funerals; they affect what holidays we celebrate and how. The importance of bar mitzvah, baptism, and other sacraments and rites depends on one's religion. Perhaps most important, our religion largely influences our values. Our religion informs what we see as right and wrong, how we view life after death, and what one must do in this life to fare well in the next.

All these influences affect our—and our children's—sense of identity and heritage. When one of our adult children changes or ignores his religion, often it sparks tension between us.

The number one question in the minds of parents experiencing religious conflict with their children is: "What shall I do now?" There are only two basic choices: Abandon them, rejecting them because you disagree with their choice; or relate to them, keeping the doors of communication open.

The wise parent will choose the second option. Learn to process your own frustration and learn to talk with—and listen to—your child in a noncontrolling manner.

A Different Approach

Parents may be presented by any number of scenarios when their children do not conform to the religious tradition in which they were raised. Naomi was Jewish, but her daughter Sara had been invited to a Christian church while in college and liked it. Naomi thought Sara would grow out of this "phase," but she was hurt, then angry, and finally livid when Sara told her that she had accepted Jesus as her Messiah and had been baptized in the Christian church.

Gio had grown up in a nominal Christian home and roomed with a Hindu from India as a college freshman. He became fascinated with Hinduism, and by the end of the school year, Gio announced to his astonished parents that he had decided to become a Hindu.

"Mom was devastated when I chose a different religious tradition," Grace said. "It was a very hard time for both of us. When she was older and moved in with me, I would go with her to the early service at her place of worship to honor her and later to my own."

Allen's twentysomething single son and daughter had been raised in the denomination with a liturgical-type service their family had belonged to for generations. Allen was taken aback when both of his adult children preferred a nondenominational church, which they described as having lively music and relevant sermons. He had heard about those contemporary-type churches and was uncomfortable at what he perceived was a lack of structure.

Open but noncondemning dialogue offers the potential to further influence the young person's thinking.

If parents are harsh, condemning, and rigid, they lose the opportunity to influence their child's future thinking. The young person sees his parents as out of touch and refuses to discuss religious matters with them. If parents can be accepting of their child's freedom to explore other religions or worship styles and will openly discuss the merits of other belief systems, they will also have the opportunity to share what they perceive to be the inconsistencies or detrimental practices of these religions. Open but noncondemning dialogue offers the potential to further influence the young person's thinking. However, angry, explosive statements of condemnation shut down the possibility of further communication.

As a parent, you may be deeply troubled with your child's religious interest. However, you must not forfeit your future influence or relationship by dogmatically condemning your child for having such interests. Since a young adult is in the process of developing his or her own beliefs, it will help you to realize that this is a normal part of the developmental transition to adulthood. Children may express interest in several world religions before settling into their own belief system. If you can walk with them through this process by reading about these religions and talking openly with them, you can be an influential part of this process. But if you condemn the pursuit, your children must walk alone or choose other mentors.

Allen spoke with his rector, who wisely reminded him that "many young adults explore different religious options. They are developing their own self-identity, and religion is one area in which this emerging independence is evidenced." The rector also reminded him that a sincere faith cannot be inherited. Allen said to his children, "I've been thinking about this church thing, and I've decided I trust each of you to make your own choices for something so personal. I won't bug you about it anymore. And one of these days, I'll come out your way and go to church with you. How would that be?"

Allen realized he should be glad his children were in church at all, since many young people were calling themselves "nones"[20] and not embracing religion at all.

"Faith Unbundled"

One researcher found a trend he dubbed "faith unbundled." Upon interviewing young adults, researchers found various responses to why some are not identifying with or pursuing a traditional religion, especially when they were raised in a religious family.[21] "I don't feel safe within religious or faith institutions," "I don't trust religion, faith, or religious leaders," "I don't feel like I need to be connected to a specific religion" were some typical statements.

Something anyone of an older generation who has a nonreligious young adult in their life may consider is a "spiritual siblinghood."[22] Such a relationship could come from the young adult's parents, but also from a coworker or other person. Enjoying authentic conversation over coffee can promote a friendship that could certainly lead to open and intentional sharing about the young adult's thinking about faith matters. Concerned parents of an adult child can look around and enlist someone to be a "spiritual sibling" to their son or daughter.

And Then There Were Nones

We've looked at Naomi, the Jewish mother whose daughter chose Christianity; Allen, whose twentysomething children preferred a different type of worship than his; and Gio's parents, whose college-aged son explored a religion quite different from their own. These young adults were exploring while they were in early adulthood. But how can religious parents react when their adult children who are at a more established age opt to not attend religious services or practice any religion at all?

If your son or daughter is questioning or even rejecting the faith they were raised with, realize that this isn't the end of the road. Try not to be critical or preachy. Openly live out your beliefs, showing their reality through your life. If you have made mistakes while your child was growing up, admit it. It is never too late to say, "I realize that when you were growing up, my lifestyle did not demonstrate very well what I claimed to believe. In more recent days, I've changed my thinking and behavior in many areas and wish I could go back and live parts of my life again. Of course, that's impossible, but I want you to know that I regret the way I failed you. I hope we'll have opportunity to share with each other something of our personal beliefs and practices in the future." Such honest and vulnerable sharing of your heart has the potential of creating a fresh climate of openness between the two of you.

You can seek common ground rather than argue. Affirm their "commitment to logic and reason and willingness to wrestle with tough questions and have difficult conversations." You might even tell them you respect "their courage in facing life and all of its hardships without a belief in an eternal life or a loving and forgiving God."[23] Be open about your own beliefs and be able to explain how and why you've come to believe as you do. Someone has described the journey to faith, or back to faith, as a marathon and not a sprint.[24] Don't expect a quick turnaround to your adult child's decision to not practice a religion, but don't give up talking and praying either. And, as with so many things we're discussing in this book, don't be afraid to wisely and with discretion share your struggles and concerns with other parents of adult children. You'll find much common ground there!

GAMING

Gaming is an area that can cause issues for adults, so parents of adult children should be aware of these and know when to step in.

Many people enjoy using their phone or other device to play video games. The Entertainment Software Association reports that about 65 percent of Americans play video games, and three-quarters of players are over eighteen. The average age of a video game player in the United States is thirty-two.[25] With over 216 million people playing each week, it's hardly an uncommon activity, and even has some cognitive benefits. People play to pass the time, to unwind after a long day at work, to stimulate their mind, or just because it's enjoyable.

However, is there a point when this activity gets hold of a person and they're unwilling or feel unable to stop? Though many people enjoy this activity, a gamer is described as "a hobbyist who plays interactive games, especially video games . . . and who plays for unusually long periods of time."[26] Such attention to this activity distracts from typical concerns of daily life and can even create a complex world in which one immerses himself. Gamers often make connections with other gamers online even though they are not physically present with one another. "Virtual social interaction often serves as a surrogate for face-to-face human connection."[27]

"I like video games," Jay explains. "A lot of my friends do too. We like to get away from the daily grind, and virtually meet up with others. It's a way to feel connected with others with similar interests, but without the drama of real-life relationships." Jay continued, explaining that games, with their increasingly complex graphics, become more and more mesmerizing. "The trouble is that playing can give you a feeling that you've really accomplished something, when in reality that feeling of satisfaction is just fake. My friends—and me too for a while—spend more time honing their virtual skills than they do on improving real-life useful skills or character development."

Jay added that video games can be a safe space, one in which the gamer has control. He doesn't need to deal with real-world challenges or disappointments because he can withdraw to a virtual world where he needn't interact much with others in day-to-day ordinary situations. He can compete through the world of gaming and succeed, where he may not be so successful in his workplace. He may develop a rapport with other gamers but struggle socially apart from the virtual world.

When It Becomes a Problem

Only about 4 percent of gamers qualify as having an addiction to this habit, or a gaming disorder,[28] so most people can enjoy video games without it becoming a problem. How can parents determine if their adult child is addicted to gaming, or if there are other factors at play in his or her life? If you think there is a gaming problem, ask yourself these questions:

Does she spend a lot of time thinking about games even when she is not playing, or planning when she can play next? When she is unable to play, is she restless, irritable, moody, angry, anxious, bored, or sad? Has she realized she should play less, but is unable to cut back?

Does he pursue more and more exciting games? Does he need more powerful equipment to reach the level of excitement he once found? Has he curtailed his participation in other recreational activities because of his involvement in gaming?

Has he deceived others about how much time he spends gaming?

Is she gaming to escape from other problems, such as stress in the workplace or school, or disappointment in relationships?

Has your adult child lost relationships, educational, or career opportunities because of gaming? Has your child's health been affected? Has there been weight gain from inactivity? Weight loss from skipping meals? Back pain due to sitting still for long periods of time?[29]

How Should Parents Respond?

If your child is still a teen, you can learn tools to help her use the screen in a healthy way. You have the right and ability to enforce screen-time boundaries in your home. You may need the help of a counselor to delve deeper and determine why your child is spending so much time in the virtual world, and also work to develop a more effective relationship with your child.

But what if your adult child is older, and should be well into living a responsible life and independent life?

"My son is twenty-eight. He was a good enough student through high school, but he has not been able to hold a job that would provide a living wage, so he lives with me," Mike, a divorced father, lamented. "Almost all he seems to do is play video games alone in his room. Is that like being some sort of addict?"

Dinah said, "My son is thirty-three and refuses to work or get an education. I realize that some young people just take longer to bloom, but this is ridiculous. He plays video games all the time. He never goes out, doesn't have friends, and just isn't living what I'd call a normal life. My husband is ready to throw him out. What can I do?"

Ellen's daughter, Emmie, left her husband because he was addicted to video games. After just three years of marriage, the relationship broke up because Emmie felt her husband cared more about interacting with strangers on his cellphone than with her. Now Ellen is trying to help her heartbroken daughter put her life back together.

These parents and countless others know the sting of addiction to gaming. Some more severe situations may require the help of a professional, especially when underlying reasons have contributed to or exacerbated the addiction.

When It's Time to Confront

Mike decided it was time to confront his twenty-eight-year-old son, Jerry. He was fortunate that Jerry was ready to try to deal with his addiction and make changes in his own life, but he was having a difficult time. Prodded by Jerry's willingness, Mike suggested they do some research together about the situation and what could be done. They learned that, as with other addictions, there is a physical response to playing video games, which will need to be fed. The Mayo Clinic explains that "if a person experiences hyperarousal while playing video games, the brain associates the activity with dopamine. The person develops a strong drive to seek out that same pleasure again and again."[30] So Mike suggested Jerry attempt going without video games for short segments of time: one morning to start with, then half a day, then full days, and so on. Jerry was not always successful, but it was a start, and he was willing to try.

After a couple of weeks, Mike removed the main internet connection from Jerry's room and installed it in his own and locked the door. He knew Jerry was slipping out to find other venues where he could access the internet but hoped that the additional effort that it took would begin to deter him. He was wise enough to recognize that something else would have to take the place of gaming in order for Jerry to mature and become independent not only from gaming but toward a meaningful life. He suggested activities they could do together, and the two joined a bowling league. They also together took a cooking class and enjoyed experimenting at home with the new cuisine they were learning.

"When Jerry's mom and I split up," Mike explains, "Jerry stayed with me. That's been ten years. I don't think he ever quite got over our breakup. Maybe in an unhealthy way I didn't encourage him to spread his wings and take off like other kids his age. Maybe I didn't want to be alone." Mike took the courageous step of seeking family counseling for himself and, after a time, Jerry agreed to go with him. Together they each better understood their own needs, and Jerry was eventually able to articulate how gaming was fulfilling for himself needs that would be better filled in healthier ways.

It wasn't an easy road for Jerry to break his addiction to gaming, but he did. He went through some typical withdrawal symptoms: irritability, sleeplessness, restlessness. He was angry at first when Mike explained that it was time for him to get and hold a job and contribute to the household. Mike made and enforced the difficult decision to give Jerry a deadline for becoming employed after which he would no longer be able to live in the home. Jerry did find a job he enjoyed, though, and work gave him and Mike something else in common they could talk about.

"Our story has a happy ending," Mike relates. "I guess my own guilt and loneliness after the breakup went on too long, and I was enjoying having Jerry at home with me. I overlooked his growing addiction to gaming until I woke up and realized the hold it had on him."

Jerry adds, "I see now that I was growing more and more antisocial, finding my friends anonymously online. Now I work in a restaurant where I meet plenty of people, both customers and staff. It turns out I'm pretty good with people, and I'm learning the restaurant business. I'm taking a class at the community college and learning about business management. I don't know how it'll all turn out, but for now, I'm content and hopeful for the future. I'm lined up to move into an apartment next month. And Dad's ready for me to go," he added with a grin.

> Joanna said, "It sounds a little simplistic, but I suggested that my daughter write out a list each morning of things to do besides play video games. I joined her by writing out what I could do instead of reaching for a snack."

MONEY: WOES AND WISDOM

Your adult child may be caught in financial woes, whether through poor choices, massive student debt, or just not earning a good living wage. Some are in a trap because of over- or irresponsible spending. They want money to buy things and to have fun. From high-end jeans to frequent dining out to the latest tech offerings, many young adults are using credit cards and big loans to gain lots of goods. They are caught in consumerism.

To be fair, some parents have chased this materialistic dream too, and we have passed it on to our offspring. We regret what we taught, but now our adult children mimic us.

Unfortunately, consumerism hinders an adult child's independence in many ways. Indeed, worries and stress over debt have become battlefields in many young adult marriages, and in many not-so-young marriages also. Failure to discuss debt with a prospective marriage partner can set up the marriage for deceit and ultimately failure. When possessions become more important than people, relationships inevitably suffer. Meanwhile, single adults often find themselves so far in debt that they see no way out, and such an attitude fosters depression.

The false idea that one can "have it all" reflects immature thinking. The reality is we cannot have everything we want. Delayed gratification is one of the signs of maturity, yet consumerism has become bondage for many young adults.

Model Responsibility

Many young people, whether married or not, face adulthood with very high debt levels, part of it for their education but another large part for purchases on credit. They have no realistic plan for

An advice columnist received the following letter: "I'm a 29-year-old still living at home. I want to go back to school and get my master's degree. It would be cheaper to do it online, but if I lived on campus I could get my own apartment and have more privacy. I believe my mental health would improve because my parents drive me crazy. However, I probably won't be able to afford to go on vacations since my financial aid will go mostly to room and board. What should I do?"[31]

paying off their debts, which can reach a staggering amount.

Parents can help their children escape consumerism several ways. Don't automatically bail out your adult children. When they face their dilemma, some young adults call on their parents for financial aid. If you have done this in the past, it is not too late to change your ways. You can admit to your child, "I realize that I have failed in my efforts to help you learn how to handle finances. I had plenty and wanted to share with you, but I've done it in a way that has made you dependent on me. That is not a good position for you. I know that you want to be self-sufficient, and I apologize that I haven't helped you reach that goal earlier. I want us to rethink what we are doing and find a way for you to learn how to live on a budget that is within your grasp. What are your thoughts about this?"

Whether we realize it or not, most of us have deep feelings about helping financially. Some of us feel adamantly that everyone should be able to "make it on his own" and that it is immature to seek help from parents. Others, usually without realizing it, are so anxious for their offspring that they find it hard to say no. Either extreme can be harmful; there are appropriate times and situations for helping an adult child, but we must take care in how and when we do so.

When your child requests financial assistance, you should not rush to conclusions but listen to the whole story. Depending on the situation, it may be appropriate and loving to help financially. Ask questions to make sure you understand the request and also to assure your child that you care. If you jump to a decision, or sound as if you have, you run the risk of making a mistake and also hurting your child. In most decisions about money, it is wise to delay, giving yourself time to think it over. It takes time to think, and even more time to discuss the matter with your spouse. Both parents must feel good about the decision that is made. This is another occasion to pray about the matter, for wisdom and a sense of peace.

After you have given the matter sufficient thought and prayer, you can give a reasonable reply to the request. If your answer is not what your adult child wanted, you need to make sure that you do not argue about your decision. You'll want to be understanding, pleasant, and firm, and also avoid being manipulated. Give your answer, your reasons, and then move on to something else. If appropriate, you can consider advising your child on other possible ways to meet the need.

When You Decide to Help

If you decide that you want to lend or give your child some money, be careful in the way you manage the loan or gift, so that the real need is met and the financial situation of you and your spouse and also of the young person is not put in jeopardy. Even with your adult child, it is usually a good idea to have the terms of a loan agreement on paper and a signature affixed. Most financial advisers warn against lending large amounts of money to adult children, especially those on the younger side of adulthood. Many such loans would never be made by banks because the young adult cannot demonstrate the ability and has limited resources to repay the loan. When parents grant a loan, they put the young adult child in a no-win situation; the child will likely be unable to repay the loan and, when the nonpayment occurs, it inevitably creates ill will between parents and the child.

Many young people ask favors instead of money—favors that give them a monetary advantage. The most common are in the area of childcare or work on their home. You need to be fully comfortable with what you agree to do for them. Otherwise, resentment will build on your part and the requests will continue on theirs.

In all your dealings with your children about finances or favors, keep in mind that you should do nothing that will threaten your long-term relationship. You don't want a conflict to harm the quality of family life now or for the future. Remember, the goal is always to bring your adult children to independence and maturity.

Colin and June

Ron and Cyndi's son Colin had a car that was constant trouble. It needed one minor repair after another, repairs Colin was able to handle. But when the need for major work arose, he went to his father for help. Together, with the advice of a trusted mechanic, they decided the car was worth repairing. Colin paid what he could, and Ron made up the rest. Ron told Colin he considered the amount a gift rather than a loan. Colin had a responsible job and, unlike his older sister June, had a history of living within his means.

Two years later, Colin's car breathed its last. He determined it was time for either a new vehicle or a quality used one, and he started hunting. He did his research, both by asking around among his friends and going online to glean from others' experiences. He found what he was looking for and at a good price—but even with a trade-in, the down payment was beyond his means and the monthly payments plus insurance would be a stretch, though doable.

She expected to impress her parents by adding, "The new jacket I bought last year will be good enough."

Again, he approached his dad. Ron worked with Colin to create a plan to help him with the down payment, but this time it wouldn't be a gift. It would be a loan, and Colin agreed.

Ron and Cyndi's other child, June, also asked for money. Encouraged by Colin's arrangement, she approached her parents and requested a conference, presenting her desire as a business matter. She too had done some research and was prepared with facts: she informed Ron and Cyndi that 68 percent of parents make financial sacrifices to help their adult children.[32] Her needs were simple: she needed new furniture in the apartment she shared with two other young women, and she needed a vacation. She and her roommates were planning a ski trip and had consulted a travel agent. "You wouldn't believe the deal he found for us!" June explained that she wouldn't even need too many new clothes, and expected to impress her parents by adding, "The new jacket I bought last year will be good enough."

Ron and Cyndi had a different take on the situation. June's job working for an uncle was sufficient if she lived sensibly, but it wasn't necessarily a position with a future. They knew from her social media posts that she ate out often. Her furniture was what they had given her when she moved out. Before giving her an answer about her request, they asked her to go over her budget with them and show them what steps she was taking to cut down on her spending. Making coffee at home instead of stopping each morning for a gourmet beverage was one thing they mentioned.

Ron and Cyndi helped June see where she could sensibly cut expenses. Could she take a bus instead of ride share? Could she cut out two or more of her streaming services? Could she try one change per month and commit to an amount to save? They helped her see that by setting a goal of where she'd like to be in, say, six months, she should be able, with self-discipline, to save up for a ski vacation the next year.

June was disappointed and a little angry that her parents turned down her request. After all, they had helped Colin. But as Ron explained, "The situations are different. We love you and Colin equally but loving you both doesn't mean we treat you identically."

Ron and Cyndi wisely knew that sometimes "helping" is actually hurting.

eight

Becoming an In-Law and a Grandparent

When your child marries, the relationship you have had is bound to change as you move to embrace his or her spouse and welcome them as a member of your family. These extended connections can bring you great happiness, or they can rain on your parade. The outcome is partly determined by your response to them.

After your child decides to marry, you acquire a new title: in-law. Not only do you have a son- or daughter-in-law who directly influences your child, but you also become related to people who will indirectly influence your adult child as they continue to influence their own married child. In addition, you may one day have another title—grandparent—and you will share your grandchildren with your son- or daughter-in-law's parents. And, if your son or daughter chooses to marry someone who already has children, you become instant grandparents.

Just after Cole completed his apprenticeship and certified to work as an electrician, he married Alma. The two had dated for a couple of years, fallen in love, and looked forward to becoming husband and wife. While Cole was studying for his license, Alma had lived at home with her parents and handled insurance claims for a dental practice. Cole secured a job with a company in his hometown.

The couple found and furnished an apartment and anticipated that their first year of marriage would be the happiest of their lives. Unfortunately, it turned out to be the most painful.

Their conflicts centered around Alma's parents. To put it in Cole's words, "She is married to them. I'm just a boyfriend. If it's convenient to be with me, fine; but her parents come first."

Alma insisted that this was not true. "Of course Cole is number one in my life, but I also want a good relationship with my parents. Is something wrong with that? I don't think I should have to choose between them." She did acknowledge that there had been times when she and Cole had plans; then her parents would call, and she would change their plans to accommodate them. This infuriated Cole.

Rollis and Deanne, Cole's parents, were aware of the difficulties. "Mom, I know you invited us over for dinner tonight, but this afternoon, Alma got a call from her mother asking if we could come over and stay with her brother who is sick," Cole explained. This was not an untypical occurrence. "Her parents have a business engagement and don't want to leave David alone. Alma told them we would come. I'm not very happy about this," Cole added. "David is definitely old enough to stay by himself for a few hours, but Alma feels that we'd be letting her parents down if we didn't go. I hope you guys understand."

"Of course," Deanne answered. "That's fine. We can do it another time." As she tried to be reassuring, she could tell by Cole's tone of voice that this was a bigger problem than simply keeping Alma's sick brother company. Her apprehensions were realized a month later when Cole was sitting at her table.

"Mom, I don't know how to tell you this, but this thing with Alma's parents is causing serious problems. Her parents are so demanding, and she doesn't know how to stand up to them. Or she doesn't want to. Whatever they ask, she does. They're trying to control us, and I'm tired of it. They are so different from you and Dad. I had no idea that they were so demanding or that they would require so much of Alma's time. She's working four days a week, and her Fridays off and a lot of Saturdays are spent doing things for them."

Deanne listened carefully and let Cole finish.

"Her mother treats her as though she was still living at home and we weren't even married. She acts hurt if Alma doesn't go shopping with her every time she calls. She is very manipulating and tries to make Alma feel it's practically a sin if she doesn't do everything her mother wants. I thought Alma was stronger than that, but I guess I was wrong. I've talked with her, but she doesn't hear what I'm saying. She thinks I want her to abandon her folks. That's not it at all. I just want her to be my wife first and their daughter second."

Deanne's Reaction

Now, what would you do if your son or daughter had a marital problem and shared the situation with you? How would you get involved—if at all? For Deanne, she wanted to tell Cole that everything was going to be all right as she had when he was a little boy. But he wasn't a child anymore, and this pain wasn't like a skinned knee. She knew she couldn't solve his marital problems, but she did have a perspective she decided to share with him.

"I appreciate your telling me this. I know it is serious and is causing you a lot of pain. I also know that in the first year of marriage, many couples have similar problems. Those who make it deal with their problems in a realistic way. The couples who don't make it are the ones who sweep their problems under the rug, trying to act as if they don't exist. In reality, problems just get larger."

Cole nodded.

"Sharing this with me is a first step," Deanne said. "Now I want to encourage you to take a second. I'm not the one to give you marriage counseling, but that's what you and Alma need. There is a counselor on our church staff; and I also know two good ones in town. If money is a problem, Dad and I can help. The important thing is that both of you talk to someone with skills in helping couples work through such difficulties. Don't let it go on or it will just get worse."

Cole replied, "I don't know if she'll go. She'd be really upset if she knew I was talking to you about this."

"Then perhaps you can tell her that you are going for counseling because you need help in dealing with your own struggle," his mother answered, "and that you would like her to go with you. You can leave me out of it. She may go because she wants the counselor to hear her side of the story. But if she doesn't, just go alone. At least you will get the process started and she may join you later. Your problem isn't going to go away by itself, and you need someone to help you work through it."

Cole agreed, and when he drove home, he felt better than when he had come. At least he knew the first step to take.

Alma was reluctant, but she did go with Cole to the counselor, and in the months that followed, they both learned a great deal about how to meet each other's needs and build an authentic marriage. Not only did Alma have an unhealthy relationship with her parents, especially her mother, but Cole was intent on proving himself in his job, which took up a lot of his mental and emotional energy. Through counseling he realized he was failing to meet Alma's emotional need for love. She desired quality time with him, but his job was so demanding that she often spent her evenings alone. She had finally decided that she might as well be with her mother rather than stay home by herself.

During months of counseling, they came to understand each other better and made some significant changes. Alma began to respond differently to her parents' requests, particularly when she and Cole had already made plans. Cole learned how to meet Alma's need for love and to make more time for her. They have now been married five years and have a mutually fulfilling relationship.

Deanne's Wise Advice

Thus your response to these new relationships can bring you happiness or heartache, joy or jealousy. Cole's mother was extremely wise in her responses to her son's complaint about his wife. In her counsel we can find several positive principles on how we parents can respond to the marital difficulties experienced by many young adults.

First, she took the problem seriously. She didn't brush it off by saying, "Oh, it can't be that bad. You're just overreacting. Take her out to dinner and she'll be all right." She didn't say, "Why don't you just talk to Alma about this? I'm sure if she realized what you're feeling, she would change." Nor did she suggest, "Just give her some time and be patient. I'm sure it will all work out." The fact is that marital problems don't "just work out." Our high divorce statistics are stark reminders that problems unattended get worse. As concerned parents, we should respond to signs of marital problems.

Second, she did not take sides. You can become involved without saying one spouse (usually your child) is right and the other is wrong. You don't have all the facts, and to take sides could alienate the other spouse. Note that Deanne didn't tell Cole it was his fault. Nor did she blame Alma for giving in to her mother. Instead, she remained neutral. Seldom can the responsibility for marital conflict be laid at the feet of one partner; generally, both husband and wife have done and said things to compound the problem. Both need insight into the dynamics of their relationship and then need to learn to take corrective steps in creating a different climate in which their conflicts can be resolved. When parents take sides, they only add to the problems.

Wise parents do not seek to solve the problems of their married children. They are there to make loving suggestions if these are asked for, but they do not impose themselves on their children's lives.

Third, she waited until Cole came to her for advice. As a parent, be willing to give advice but wait until such counsel is requested. Deanne might have rushed in with suggestions after she first sensed something was wrong. However, had she offered advice then, Cole might have become defensive and then not turned to her later for help. The best guideline is to wait until your married children ask for help. At that point, they are more likely to follow your suggestions.

Fourth, she offered a course of action that was specific and doable. As parents, we can give recommendations, but we should be specific. Depending on the situation, you may recommend professional counseling, seeing a financial planner, setting up a budget, getting away for a weekend. Deanne recommended counseling; she also removed the possible hurdle of the cost of counseling by offering to help. While she didn't force Cole into action, she told him why she believed it would be wise.

Also, Deanne talked with her husband about her conversation with Cole. The two determined that their relationship with the young couple would continue just as it had been. No questions, no blame, no changed attitudes toward Alma or her parents. Wise parents do not seek to solve the problems of their married children. They are there to make loving suggestions if these are asked for, but they do not impose themselves on their children's lives. They give their children space to build their own lives. They allow them the freedom to say no to invitations or requests that conflict with their plans or wishes. They relate to their children in ways that will foster their growth as individuals and as a couple.

As a parent and an in-law, your goal should be to support your child and his or her mate. Welcome your son- or daughter-in-law into the family with open arms. When asked, give advice. You'll always remain a parent; become a friend.

CONGRATULATIONS, YOU'RE A GRANDPARENT! NOW WHAT?

When your children marry, you know that you may become a grandparent someday. You may even yearn for it, to hold a grandchild in your arms, play games—and then say goodbye to parenting at the end of the day. If the years stretch on too long, some not-yet grandparents have been known to prod, to make clumsy jokes about babies, and otherwise express their eagerness to have the next generation in tow.

How important is grandparenting? A study from YouGov found that about 69 percent of Americans believe it's important for grandparents and grandchildren to be close.[1] More than half of American adults have fond memories of their grandparents, specifically mentioning holidays, family history, or learning about cultural traditions.[2] I agree that the bond between grandparent and grandchild is very important, and it's the grandparents who need to nurture that bond. If we do not take this responsibility and privilege seriously, both we and our grandchildren lose.

There are more grandparents today than ever before, because people are living longer and generally have better health. In the United States it is estimated that there are nearly 70 million grandparents today, and many do not fit into a traditional stereotype as "stay at home" kinds of people. Many grandparents are still working or have returned to work after retiring from a yearslong job. About 19 percent of Americans who are at least sixty-five are employed, and 62 percent of these are full-time.[3]

Today's grandparents tend to set boundaries to protect their own way of life and may or may not be as readily available or willing as babysitters as those on old sitcoms were. They may not even live within easy driving distance of their offspring and their children, or may themselves be long divorced or remarried, adding step-grandparents to the picture.

So how do grandparents form a strong bond with their grandchildren? Some have suggested that around age ten into the teen years, children may begin to draw back from Grandma and Grandpa. This may be due to a child's personality (or the grandparents'), physical distance, lifestyle, and other factors. Yet, many grandparents are able to intentionally stay closer to their grandkids than others do. Social psychologists Merril Silverstein and Vern L. Bengtson have studied what they dub "intergenerational solidarity," and have found six factors that affect closeness. These are physical proximity, frequency of contact, grandparents' role within the family, family expectations, emotional bonding, reaching a consensus on values.[4]

Grandparents who want to stay close to their grandchildren may have to be intentional about creating and maintaining the bond. For example, if physical proximity is an issue, there are many video chat platforms to try. Even when grandparents live far from their grandchildren, it's worthwhile to make opportunities to visit: holidays are important, though not always possible. However, Christmas needn't be celebrated only on December 25; many people celebrate with extended family throughout the season. If a grandchild is performing in a school or church program, is on a sports team, is displaying an art or science project, make every effort to be there. Your presence will make an impression on your grandchild whether or not he or she acknowledges your effort at the time.

Values can be a tough area in which to find consensus when the grandchild hits that tween and beyond stage. Grandparents may not approve of the child's clothing, video games or other activities, friends, and so on. While these issues are properly in the domain of the parents, not the grandparents, Grandma and Grandpa's role is to be willing to listen. Listening with interest and respect speaks volumes.

The Heart of the Extended Family

It's said that the more things change, the more they stay the same. We might think of yesterday's grandma as baking cookies and grandpa as whittling on a stick with his pocketknife, but to-day's grandparents are more likely to be going to work and going to the gym. Still, grandparents are the heart of the extended family. Grandparents are the family historians, the ones who keep the family tied to its roots and to the past. As we get older, we become more interested in those who preceded us, and we can then share this with the younger members of the family.

> "Grandparents can be very special treasures. Just being close to them reassures a child, without words, about change and continuity, about what went before and what will come after."
> — Fred Rogers

Grandparents offer security and stability to grandchildren, and this is especially important in a time of change. They represent unconditional love, kindness, and understanding. They are nonjudgmental counselors. They can ease their sorrows and give encouragement during difficult times. They are there to encourage our children when they need us and are a refuge when stress and tension become overwhelming. They are in the best position to be their grandchildren's own cheerleaders, to get excited about each one, and lift high their self-esteem.

Grandparents can stand for spiritual guidance and strength. Many grandparents choose to pray for each grandchild as well as for their parents. They offer comfort and good cheer and become role models of a deep spiritual faith for their grandchildren. Israel's King Solomon wrote, "Children's children are a crown to the aged."[5] Yes, grandchildren are special gifts.

Because our role with them is different than with anyone else, our grandchildren regard us differently than they do anyone else. Because of this, we can employ those bonds to give them strength, courage, and faith as they grow. It is definitely our choice how we use our special powers to influence for good these wonderful grandchildren who have come into our lives.

Two Truths About Grandkids

All grandparents should remember these two truths about grandchildren: 1. They are *not* your children; and 2. They *are* your grandchildren.

The first truth seems obvious, and yet forgetting it can cause untold problems. Because you are not their parents, you should never overstep the right and authority of the parents. This means that you need to consult their parents before you give or loan them money, take them to events, or make extravagant plans. Similarly, talk to the parents before you give the grandchildren major advice. Your failure to respect parental authority can create extreme conflict between you and your adult children.

Whether you live close by or at some distance, you need to remember that the children are constantly growing and changing. Be sensitive and alert to their needs.

One common point of difference today is in the means of disciplining children. It is important that you know the goals and guidelines your children are employing as they raise their children. Discuss discipline with them if you like, but do not ignore their policies or try to change them. Respect your children's role as parents. If you and they work together to make the world of the growing children one of delight and security, you will be drawn closer in the bonds of family love.

The second truth also is quite obvious: they are your grandchildren, and you have an important, loving role to play. Yet it takes imagination and continuing time and contact to make your role work for you and your grandchildren. You have certain emotional and legal rights to these children, of course, but exercising these rights needs to be done with the greatest care, since you want to build a lifelong relationship with these special children. Just as you think of them in the warmest way, so you want them to regard you with particular affection.

> "I believe in kindness. Also in mischief. Also in singing, especially when singing is not necessarily prescribed."
> — Mary Oliver, "Evidence"

Whether you live close by or at some distance, you need to remember that the children are constantly growing and changing. Be sensitive and alert to their needs; consult their parents for a better understanding of their abilities and interests, especially if you are not able to visit them regularly. You may be anticipating something wonderful that you want to do with or give to your grandchild, only to discover that the toy you so carefully selected is not right for his age, or that she is fully absorbed in another pursuit. You may have in mind a trip you want to share with a grandchild and may need to recognize that what an adult thinks is intriguing may be far beyond a child's interests.

Something all grandparents can share is time. When you give time and attention, you are placing yourself at the child's disposal, to play, to read, to explore, and most of all to give unconditional love. This does not mean allowing the child to do everything he wishes. It does mean that you are always looking out for his best interests, that you love this child and are open in showing how you feel. You are always excused for giving the most extravagant and exuberant praise. You are among the few people who can make your grandchild glow, often with a level of silliness that you couldn't get away with anywhere else. Few relationships hold greater potential for mutual pleasure and affirmation than a loving grandparent-grandchild bond.

In sharing yourself, you are giving your grandchild your unique outlook on life, your ways, your memories, your skills and interests, and, most of all, your love. As the child grows and develops wider knowledge, this can become more significant, with long-lasting influence on the child and great satisfaction to you.

Long-Distance Grandparenting

You may be separated by geographical distance from your grandchildren, but this doesn't need to mean an emotional distance. With all the facilities of communication, it is ever easier to stay in touch. We think of letters, phone calls, and email, but there are other ways grandparents can strengthen the bond. Here are several examples of creative communication by grandparents separated by miles but seemingly next door through their regular contact:

- Eileen, a Midwestern grandma, shares books with her granddaughter in Florida. She buys two copies of the same book or ebook and sends one to Taryn. They read the same chapter each week, and on the weekend, Grandma calls Taryn on the phone to talk with each other about the story—what they liked or didn't like. This can lead to interesting discussions about Taryn's feelings and sometimes about life itself. These two could be reading buddies for life.

- Each month Chet composes a short story and emails it to his great-granddaughter in California. Marli downloads it and later responds to her great-grandpa, along with her comments or questions. Some of Chet's stories are true accounts from his own life and others are fiction. Lately he's started writing about some of his ancestors so when Marli reaches the age of becoming interested in people from the past, she'll have some facts and anecdotes stored up.

- Sue has a weekly date to video chat with Aly and Abby, now tweens.

- Lynn's young grandsons Ezra and Levi live in another state. She says, "I started video recording stories. Now I can 'read' to them before naps or bedtime, even when I'm hours away."

- "How much longer till we spend a week with Mamaw and Papaw?" eight-year-old Aaron asked. It was the highlight of his summer to spend a week on his grandparents' farm in Iowa, something he had been doing since he was five. It was the only time his grandparents saw him each year, and so Mamaw Lora would take pictures of their week together and put them on Facebook. After Aaron returned home, he would be just a click away from reliving vacation memories.

Creative grandparents always find ways to stay in touch and express their love to grandchildren separated by the miles. This may involve buying stickers and sending them to a granddaughter who has a collection or purchasing baseball cards or caps for another. Anything that says "We are thinking about you" strengthens the bond. As mentioned before, it is wise to check with the parents to be sure the gift is appropriate and welcome.

One cardinal rule of effective grandparenting, whether from a distance or just across town, is to treat all grandchildren in an equitable manner. One child could be especially appealing to a grandparent. That's understandable. You may like the child's age, appearance, or behavior. However, it is crucial that you show love and attention as equally as you can. Even into adulthood, people never forget when grandparents obviously favored one child in a family over the others, and this can cause conflict among the siblings. Also, the favored one knows that something is out of kilter and does not appreciate the favoritism in the way the grandparents might imagine. If you are having difficulty understanding or appreciating the special qualities of each grandchild, *The 5 Love Languages of Children* is a great resource.[6]

These principles about favoritism apply to stepchildren or adopted children as well. If you treat them as you do your own flesh and blood, you may be happily surprised to find that in time you feel close to them.

Grandparenting When Your Children Divorce

Divorce is one of the most crushing and destructive experiences a person can go through, and it does not disappear if he or she remarries. Divorce deeply affects children. Many children believe that they are responsible for their parents' divorce—if they had been better, their parents would have stayed together. Hurt, anger, and insecurity are the most common emotions felt by these children. In all their pain, grief, and disillusionment, they can find solace in grandparents who are available with comforting arms.

But a word of caution: Grandparents often are experiencing their own pain, even grief, because of their children's divorce, and grandparents must learn to control their own emotions in order to help their grandchildren. When their world seems to be falling apart, these children reach for emotional support—that is, if the grandparents can retain a distance from the conflicts of the children's parents. In some cases, one set of grandparents is of no help to the children, because they are so heavily invested in blaming. At such a time, the children of whatever age should be the first consideration.

As grandparents, we need to recognize that we cannot solve the marital problems of our children, but we can love and care for our grandchildren. A listening ear, a caring hug, a prayer, and just being there all tell your grandchildren, "We care." Our grandchildren need to know that Grandma and Grandpa will be there for them, that we love them, and that we and our feelings won't change. They also need to know that their parents both still love them and always will. As grandparents, we are in the best position to bring this assurance to them.

The important role for grandparents is to be loving, caring, assuring, and giving of full attention.

In the midst of divorce, our grandchildren may bring questions to us. Answering these questions is usually difficult because we need to use caution. It is helpful to remember that most children don't want specific answers, but just want to express their feelings in a safe place. And yet, we can't ignore direct questions about the parents and the divorce. It is wisest to give the least possible amount of information. If they ask again, give just a tiny amount more. Also, there are some questions that only the parents should answer. The important role for grandparents is to be loving, caring, assuring, and giving of full attention.

While you may be concentrating on your grandchildren, you are clearly concerned for your son or daughter who is going through the divorce. You may be angry at what you consider to be their wrong behavior, or you may feel sympathetic because of "the way they have been treated." In most divorces, the blame is not all on one side. Both partners have likely failed in their efforts to understand and to give unconditional love to each other. Most misbehavior in marriage grows out of an empty love tank. Many spouses have never learned how to meet each other's need for love. When this goes unmet, we tend to be our worst selves.

While you cannot solve your children's problems or be a marriage counselor, you can recommend counseling and perhaps pay for it. You can make available some resources that may help them put things back together. Two books that many couples have found especially helpful are *One More Try: What to Do When Your Marriage Is Falling Apart* and *The 5 Love Languages.*

When Your Children Remarry

Many family circles are enlarging as young adults marry for the second time, and even for the third, bringing new children into grandparents' lives. With 80 percent of divorced people remarrying, many grandparents are finding that someone new is now helping raise the grandchildren. As a grandparent, you have a concern for your grandchildren's well-being, yet at the same time must realize that your adult children have to be free to make their own decisions. Once your son or daughter has chosen to remarry, you need to accept that decision and seek to relate positively to the new spouse. If children from a former marriage are present, the new spouse has also become a new stepparent.

Even in the best of stepfamily situations, there is bound to be some tension, as the children are divided in their loyalties and are trying to adjust to new authority figures and siblings. Children may blame the new stepparent for all their problems, from the failure of the first marriage to the remarriage, and the confusion of moving. Also, children may blame their own parent for the breakup of their home, and also for marrying someone new. Grandparents can be points of stability and comfort when children are going through hard times.

Grandparents are often in the best situation to provide the emotional and even spiritual nurturance the children need.

Sometimes a grandparent receives signals that suggest the new stepparent is ignoring or mistreating a grandchild. The grandparent wants to intercede. If you should ever discover that the stepparent is behaving in an abusive way, you certainly have the right and responsibility to speak up on behalf of the children. But how and to whom you speak is important. It is best if your adult child can take initiative to confront the abusing spouse about the issue. Your role may be to encourage and support your child. If your child is emotionally or mentally unable to do this, you may want to contact the national center for reporting physical abuse and ask for suggestions on what action you should take.

Being a step-grandparent is not easy, and yet as such, you are in a wonderful position to help the entire family. The more cordially you can relate to the new spouse, the better it will go with your new grandkids. If you can just be relaxed and patient, your relationship with your new step-grandchildren will probably develop naturally. It is rare that a grandparent does not eventually develop a loving bond with every grandchild, step or not. One thing you can do is to get acquainted with the other grandparents of the step-grandchildren. This will foster bonds for later cooperation and can also prevent problems.

With the tremendous increase in family disruption, grandparenting and step-grandparenting has become a vital area of helping and supporting your adult child. Many grandchildren are caught in a web of change, confusion, and bewilderment with little, if any, emotional guidance. Grandparents are often in the best situation to provide the emotional and even spiritual nurturance the children need.

WHEN GRANDPARENTS RAISE THE CHILDREN

Perhaps the most unexpected situation some grandparents may encounter is when they become parents again—rearing grandchildren on a temporary or permanent basis. The US census data indicates that about "7.1 million American grandparents are living with their grandchildren under eighteen. Some 2.3 million of those grandparents are responsible for their grandchildren. About a third of grandchildren living with grandparents who are responsible for them are younger than six."[7] In addition to economic factors, other causes include divorce, death of one or both parents, parent incarceration, child abuse, teenage pregnancy, substance abuse, and addiction.[8] Many grandparents are taking their children and grandchildren into their homes after a divorce, and others have the entire responsibility for raising one or more grandchildren. Some have called these "skipped generation households."[9]

Some grandparents find purpose in having another chance at childrearing, with its challenges and rewards. But not all. Sylvie de Toledo, founder of Grandparents as Parents and author of a book by that title, said, "Grandparents who find themselves taking the place of their adult children as parents are often bewildered and depressed by how their lives have changed."

There is no doubt that these grandparents' lives are radically changed. Their empty nest fills back up, retirement dreams are postponed or forfeited, travel is put off indefinitely, leisure time may no longer exist, and their savings often dwindle. The emotional impact can also be severe, as grandparents feel trapped, powerless, frustrated, resentful, alienated, and guilty. The guilt can come from a sense that they failed in raising their own children and are now reaping the results in their grandchildren. All of this is happening at a time in their lives when they need order and stability. In some cases, the pressure can lead to depression that must be professionally treated.

> "Hold on and enjoy the ride. You will not remember it ever being this hard when you were younger and raising your first family; the money goes quick and grandkids *always* need something. But oh, the rewards will always outweigh the struggles. I would do it all over again a thousand times."[10]

Bud and Annie

Bud and Annie, both in their early fifties and happy in what was a second marriage for both, had their lives change gradually when

Annie's daughter Roma became pregnant and returned home with her newborn to live with them. The arrangement was meant to be temporary, but within a couple of months, Roma had an incident of drunk driving, and now was involved with the police, not an unusual occurrence for her.

Over the next couple of years, Roma went through a pattern of substance abuse, rehab, promises, and recurrence. Bud and Annie, especially Annie, were little Noah's caretakers. Their lives not only included the responsibilities of caring for a baby turning toddler but going to court to obtain guardianship. Roma would change her behavior and cooperate with court-ordered rehab, at one point not being allowed any contact with Noah without supervision. Then she would relapse, and the only contact Annie had with her was what she saw on Roma's social media.

By the time Noah was four, Roma was virtually out of the picture. Annie arranged for daycare, as she and Bud both held full-time jobs, enrolled him in preschool, was the one to find the character back-pack he wanted for kindergarten, and practiced sight words with him in first grade. Bud was as active and supportive grandpa as he could be, taking Noah along to run errands and playing catch in the yard.

"I resent Roma," Annie says frankly. "I love Noah, but why has she abandoned him? Why are drugs and her drug-addled friends more important than raising her child? Noah's so-called father has never been in the picture and is probably in worse shape than Roma."

Noah is fortunate in that he's being raised by loving, stable grand-parents. Still, Annie knows he'll soon wonder why his mother "is sick" and never comes around to see him. Annie and Bud have supportive extended family who also love Noah, but they know it isn't the same. The questions will only grow more difficult as Noah gets older.

Ted and Margaret

Ted and Margaret had raised their grandson Danny after their daughter—Danny's mother, who got pregnant in her teens—had sadly died at a young age in an accident. Already having raised three other children, Ted and Margaret hadn't planned on taking on another round of child-rearing. But they didn't feel there was anyone else.

Danny was always a challenge. Undisciplined at home and disruptive at school, Danny's teenage rebellion began early. Fights, smoking, drinking, marijuana, then more serious substance abuse was part of the picture. Ted emotionally disconnected. He had retired from his job and spent his time collecting and repairing small appliances. He turned the basement into his own refuge, where he spent most of his time.

Danny's life became a pattern of arrest and short-term jail sentences. When he was out, he found time for a girlfriend who bore him two children in three years. Then he was back in jail and the mother of the babies was investigated for child neglect and the children came to live with Ted and Margaret.

Again, Margaret felt she had no choice. Her other grown children were all out of state, and the idea of any of them taking in Danny's children was a nonstarter as far as they were concerned. They were busy with their own lives and families.

By this time, Margaret and Ted were well into their seventies. Someone asked Margaret what would become of the children once she and Ted were just too old to cope or otherwise unable to continue. She admitted she didn't know. Finally, a friend insisted on accompanying Margaret to see a lawyer to learn her options and put a plan in place to protect the children's future.

If you are in this situation of caring for grandchildren—even if not as drastic as that of the examples above—you should seek support. For one thing, you must ensure that legalities are clear: Is it a case where you need to prove the parent is unfit? Are you the legal guardian? What are the terms? You may look for help through a support group in your community or online. The American Association for Marriage and Family Therapy offers ideas and links to resources.[11] The AARP website (aarp.org) also has information on grandparents raising grandchildren. They may be able to assist you in locating a support group in your area and also answer questions about custody, health insurance, welfare benefits, and other issues that you face. Check back with online sources as they're often refreshed and updated.

You should feel free to ask for the help that you need, not only from government agencies but also from your church and community groups. You may find people who would be glad to volunteer some time and support that will give you a needed lift. During your later years, you can find strength to help you bring guidance and love to your grandchildren.

nine

Mending Relationships and Reconciliation

Year by year, we all face more stress. With our rapidly changing society, we need to learn to maintain ourselves better as we grow older. If we fail to give a high priority to our own well-being, we will have less energy and will feel more disillusioned. This leads to a loss of perspective about ourselves, our relationships, and life itself. Such loss of perspective can happen to any of us if we do not replenish ourselves physically, emotionally, and spiritually, as we discussed in chapter 6. Part of this self-nurture is to resolve issues that have the power to drag us down and plague us for years and even decades—issues that make us feel guilty, depressed, lonely, discouraged, or unworthy.

Those issues usually are related to the most basic elements of our lives and to the people who are or have been the closest to us. The issues often include the mistakes we have made in our own parenting. They can also include the mistakes our own parents made in their parenting of us—actions and attitudes that left us hurting with a pain that continues.

Most people have some mending to do on both sides, so a place to start is to look first to the hurts from the past. In this chapter we'll look at scenarios of ways adult children can mend relationships with their parents—and perhaps you may have issues regarding your own parents to resolve—and then briefly touch on when parents need to take measures of reconciliation with their grown children.

RETURN HOME

James's father was an angry man who was emotionally severe with his children, critical and unloving. His mother was a passive woman who simply looked on as the father raged and ranted and put her down as well. James left home right after high school graduation, glad to be away from these people. After he served four years in the army, he went to college on the GI bill and then dug into his adult life. During all these years, he went home only when necessity demanded it, such as when his sister got married.

While working on his graduate degree, James began to realize that for his own mental health he needed to mend his relationship with his parents. When he was thirty-five years old, he decided to initiate a return home simply to visit and try to repair some of the brokenness. Driving to his hometown, he thought, *Perhaps I've been too harsh toward my parents. I wonder if my reactions had merely been those of an immature teenager. I wonder . . .*

The first evening James was home, things were going well enough. As the three of them watched television together, he was feeling comfortable and thinking what a good idea coming home had been. Mom, Dad, and James were seated watching a sitcom when a woman on the show exclaimed, "This is my fifty-fifth birthday today!"

"What a coincidence," James's mother then said. "I'm fifty-five too." To which his father replied, "Yeah, but look at the difference."

He began to realize what a difficult life his father had had.

Suddenly James felt the old nauseating feelings that he hoped he had left behind. He hated his dad's cruel gibe. He realized then that mending his relationship with his parents was not going to be that easy. He nearly gave up his plan, except that he had become a Christian since leaving home and had prayed often about his painful past. James decided to stay, and the next day he engaged his father in a conversation about his own childhood.

It was an eye-opener. As they talked, James discovered that his father had had a cruel mother who physically abused him and his two siblings. He also learned that his father had been frequently ridiculed by his peers because of his exceptionally small stature. He began to realize what a difficult life his father had had. This gave him some understanding of his dad's poor self-esteem, his inability to show affection, and the smoldering anger that never entirely evaporated.

James did the same with his mother. In her case, he was surprised by the underlying intelligence that she had kept hidden beneath her retiring personality. James had never been able to respect the way his mother would not exert herself against the bad treatment of her husband. As they talked at length, he discovered that she had years before taken the civil service examination and passed it with such high scores that she was given an excellent job with the US Postal Service and became one of the first women supervisors in her area. Knowing that enabled him to respect her in a way he never had before.

That one trip, of course, did not in itself enable James to completely change his feelings and attitudes toward his parents, but it got things started. He kept in touch with them and continued to consider what he had learned about them. He prayed about his relationship with his parents and talked with his wife and close friends about it. Gradually, James gained control of his anger and resentment and eventually came to a point where thinking of his parents did not bring feelings of hurt and bitterness. This took months and was not an easy time for James.

> An old adage says, If you carry bricks from your past, you will end up building the same house.

Finally, he was able to forgive his parents for the pain that they had caused him and his sister. This had a wonderful liberating effect for James. And, best of all, it gave him a new freedom in his own parenting, so that he is now able to be and do for his children what his own parents never gave to him. And, when his parents died, he was profoundly thankful that he had dealt with those old issues while they were still alive.

It's Worth Trying

You can return home again, literally or figuratively, and you can work toward knowing your own parents better. Deeper understanding and even reconciliation are possible. There are no guarantees, of course. But an open mind and a forgiving spirit can pave the way to objectively view your past—and your parents' past.

In James's case, his conversion to Christianity resulted in a changed life and a commitment to follow Christ in all areas of his life, including trying to make peace with his feelings about his parents. Unfortunately, as a counselor, I have met adults who suffered at the hands of parents who said they were Christians. I have known numerous people whose religious parents have done many onerous acts in the name of God. This includes teaching their children, primarily by example, to scorn, blame, lie, despise, condemn, even abuse other family members. Some of these parents twist the Bible as they deal with their children, to place blame where none is due.

Can children in such relationships find healing? These are especially difficult relationships, but any effort is well worth it, for both parents and adult children. To carry a burden of anger, resentment, or bitterness is crushing and often debilitating. Finding pathways toward healing, peace, and forgiveness is a matter of grace, God's grace. It is important to God that we find that grace. Ask Him and He will help you.

ARTICULATE YOUR FEELINGS

Another way to resolve deep hurts from the past is to articulate your feelings by writing letters to your parents. The purpose of this is to get in touch with deep and possibly buried feelings. Putting those feelings on paper makes it much easier to see them accurately and then deal with them. First, you should release your negative feelings such as anger, hurt, and frustration. This may be difficult if you have suppressed them for a long time. You may be tempted to skip to positive feelings before releasing your negative ones, yet it is crucial that you be honest with yourself; everyone has some negative feelings toward their parents.

You can be fully honest with what you write. This letter should be for your own healing as you articulate your thoughts and feelings; it isn't necessarily meant to be sent. And you can take all the time you need to process those feelings that you may have forgotten. If you find yourself crying and lamenting over what happened so many years ago, go ahead and release your hurt. Perhaps your parents are no longer alive, but you still want to express your feelings.

When you have spent adequate time dealing with the negative feelings, write another letter to each parent focusing on the positive. Again, don't be in a hurry.

You may decide that one of your letters would be appropriate to actually send. Such correspondence can be a good way to communicate when distance, finances, and schedule make a return home impractical, or when you just couldn't handle a face-to-face meeting to discuss these hurts. You may find that letter writing is a good way to improve your relationship with your parents, and to keep communications positive.

Be careful to not send the correspondence until you are ready to do so; wait a while and review for tone and word choice. Spoken words can be easily misunderstood, yet written words are much easier to examine before transmission, and they're easier to talk about later. And knowing that emails can easily be forwarded, remember to be wise before communicating this way.

Receiving a Letter or a Visit

Writing a letter, whether you send it or not, can be a healing experience for you. But what if you're the parent of a grown child and you receive such a letter? Or your child confronts you in person with his or her hurts? How should you respond?

Listen to or read what he or she is saying without interrupting or correcting their perception of their experience. We may perceive the same events or patterns of daily life differently, and each person's experience with events should be validated. Do they remember the special events you missed? Do they accuse you and your spouse of too much bickering? Realize they might not know the full stories of these memories. Acknowledge their feelings and thoughts without trying to defend yourself. Where you agree with the need to apologize, do so, though you needn't apologize for things that were beyond your control.

As parents, we never intend to harm our children, but we must also remember that in most cases, we did our best with the resources—material and emotional—we had at the time. If you're having difficult conversations with your adult child, try to release your expectations of how you want him or her to react to your explanations or apologies. Your child is an adult and as an adult is responsible for his or her own response. Be as open and gracious as you can and allow time to go by for the air to clear and the relationship to improve.

CONSIDER FORGIVENESS

When you think that you have exhausted the feelings regarding your parents, at least for the time being, it is time to consider forgiving them. Yes, *consider forgiveness,* because it must be done when you are ready. It is not simply saying that you have forgiven them; it requires letting go of hurt. The act of forgiveness seldom takes place instantaneously.

As a young teen, Leigh had been sexually abused several times by a cousin who lived nearby and who was a frequent visitor to her home, as their parents were close. What happened eventually damaged her sexual relationship with her husband, and at his urging, she went for counseling and soon gained insight into how what had happened still affected her years later. Leigh knew she had to confront her parents, because when she had tried to tell them what was going on, they didn't believe her. "You're exaggerating," her father had said. "All boys are obsessed with sex. He's just teasing you. I'll tell him to cut it out and that'll be the end of it." Only it wasn't. Her mother had remained silent even when Leigh again asked for help.

When Leigh met up with her parents with the express purpose of dealing with this hurt, she told her father how the memories of those days brought her deep pain. How they had distorted her attitudes toward sex. How she had entered counseling to find help. How she was beginning to find healing. How disgusted she was that her father took her cousin's side over hers. How disappointed she was with her mother. She expressed her thoughts and feelings of resentment toward both her father and mother. Then Leigh said that she wanted to offer them forgiveness if they wanted to be forgiven.

Her parents did not instantaneously acknowledge their wrongs over the events of many years ago, but muttered apologies that day. It took a few months, but eventually they sincerely admitted their grievous shortcomings in dealing with their daughter's having been so abused. Today Leigh and her parents enjoy a cordial relationship. She is cautious about who she allows her own children to be alone with and has talked with her counselor about the possibility of confronting the cousin.[1]

But what if parents, when confronted, deny that they did anything wrong? That often happens. That was Nadine's experience. After many years, she found the courage and determination to speak to her mother about what her stepbrother had done to her, which included vicious bullying as well as being inappropriate physically. Her mother disbelieved her, accusing her of jealousy and making up a story to discredit him. Nadine provided the times and places the repeated abuse occurred and still her mother refused to listen.

Or what if parents are already deceased? You may write a letter even in that circumstance for your own healing in articulating difficult experiences and painful memories. In both cases, the approach is the same: you release them to God who judges rightly, and you release to God (who knows and understands) your anger and bitterness.[2]

RECONCILING WITH YOUR ADULT CHILD

Some parents are not fully aware of the impact their mistakes had on their children. After they realize what they have done, and that all parents have made mistakes for which they need to confess to their children (and to God), they are then able to find relief from guilt and experience the peace they have longed for.[3]

You can be the one to initiate necessary repairs. In most cases, your child will be out of the home. Therefore, the first step may be to write a letter or an email in which you express how much you love and appreciate her. You can then explain some of your problems in being the parent you wish you could have been. You may also share the mistakes you know you have made. It is here that you can ask for her forgiveness and tell her of the love you will always feel toward her.

If your child accepts your letter, it is important that the two of you talk together about the past and mend your relationship in ways that will work for the future. Of course, if your child is still at home and you are aware of a fractured relationship you have caused, you can ask for forgiveness in person. But the need to then dialogue about the past will still be necessary, and the two of you also will need to work on ways to strengthen the relationship for the future.

We cannot erase all the scars from past hurts, but we can experience freedom from the bondage of bitterness.

Regardless of the response you receive, you will know that you have done what a caring parent would do. This will ease your sorrow and guilt if your adult son or daughter rejects your heartfelt letter or personal confession and request for forgiveness. However, very few children will reject a letter of confession, remorse, and compassion. If there has been some overwhelming trauma between you and your child, it may be best to seek help from someone who is qualified to help you. You could seek professional counseling first for yourself and later, if appropriate, for other family members.

We cannot erase all the scars from past hurts, but we can experience freedom from the bondage of bitterness. Forgiveness is the higher road; it opens the way to reconciliation and closeness, and it releases us from bitterness.

Such forgiveness is taught in the New Testament, which says a Christian can and should forgive because he or she has been forgiven. The Christian message is simple: A holy, righteous God wanted to find a way to maintain His commitment to justice yet forgive the human offender. His solution was to send Jesus, who lived a perfect life and yet paid the ultimate penalty for all sin—death. Therefore, God can and does forgive all who will accept His forgiveness. Having experienced God's forgiveness, people are expected to forgive those who wrong them. The best-known prayer in the Bible includes the words "forgive us our debts, as we also have forgiven our debtors."[4] Forgiving and being forgiven for past failures gives us a new freedom to face the future unfettered by the hurt, anger, and bitterness of the past.

Have a Healthy, Positive Outlook

As you seek to increasingly relate to your child in healthy adult ways, think of the ways you relate to persons you respect and admire. You ask their opinions and discuss mutual interests with them. You invite them to activities that are important to you and to your associates. You want to move toward a healthier perspective toward life—a perspective that gives a positive mental outlook and emotional reaction to life, and especially to the future.

The way you regard the future is either more optimistic or pessimistic. You probably aren't fully in either camp but tend in one direction or the other. An optimist is more likely to ignore facts that are negative and has an overly favorable view of life. A pessimist first sees factors that are primarily negative

> "It's been my experience that you can nearly always enjoy things if you make up your mind firmly that you will."
> — Anne Shirley
> in *Anne of Green Gables*
> by Lucy Maud Montgomery

and has an overly unfavorable view of life. It is generally easier for an optimist to have a balanced perspective on life. I recommend that perspective. It will aid you in dealing with the tensions in your relationships with family and coworkers. Pessimists are more prone to depression, and that can aggravate the pessimism even more.

We have more control over our lives than we often think. We can make choices that impact us and those around us in very positive ways. We don't have to just wait and see what turns up. We don't have to feel victimized by life, even by those curveballs our children at times throw our way.

We need to be at our best for the task and privilege of parenting, at any age. Parenting adult children is just as important as parenting the little ones, but it is different, and we are learning as we go. If we want to do our best, we have to be our best.

ten

Your Legacy

It is inevitable that one generation will pass on a legacy to the next. In this chapter, we'll talk about various types of legacies and how you can be influential for your children through the ages.

Most parents arrange to leave some material legacy to their children. Sometimes the legacy can be a small but meaningful gift. Art, a fifty-four-year-old scaffold designer, buried his eighty-eight-year-old father a year after his mother passed away. His father had lived in a nursing home for several years; his money had run out, and he was on Medicaid for most of that time.

"Before he died," Art recalled, "he told me he wanted me to have his wedding ring. After his death, when I went to the nursing home, they gave me a bag with Dad's clothes. At the bottom was a small plastic bag containing his wedding ring. Now that ring is on my dresser, and I look at it every day and remind myself of Dad's faithful marriage to Mom for over fifty years. I think about all he did for me throughout my life, and I pray that I will be remembered by my family as the kind of husband and father he was." Art's words tell of a legacy far more valuable than material property.

Matt's story is very different. The only child of his widowed father, Matt received everything his father had accumulated—hundreds of thousands of dollars in cash and stocks as well two nicely furnished houses and a vintage automobile. Matt's response? "I never really knew my father and have no idea what to do with all his stuff. He left my mother and me when I was thirteen, and I didn't see him for five years. When I was ready for college, he agreed to pay for my tuition, room and board, and other expenses. From that point, we saw each other periodically over the next forty years, but we never had a close relationship. He was involved with one woman after another, and I always felt that he didn't have time for me or my own family. My children knew him only as the grandfather who gave expensive Christmas gifts.

"If I had known him, I might appreciate all the stuff he left me. Of course, I can use the money, but the inheritance doesn't have any personal meaning for me."

THE FINANCIAL LEGACY

It should be clear that the financial legacy we leave our children is far less important than the moral, spiritual, and emotional legacies. However, most people do collect a lot of "stuff" throughout their lifetime—a house, cars, furniture, clothes, books, jewelry, money, even photos and mementos. This material stuff can be a tangible way to say "I love you"; all of it will be left to others at the time of our death. And it will communicate to our children our care—or lack of it—for their welfare. The way it is left often connects with the other legacies we'll talk about, as does the response of children to what they receive.

Most parents want to pass their wealth along to their children and others. An ancient Hebrew proverb says, "A good person leaves an inheritance for their children's children, but a sinner's wealth is stored up for the righteous."[1] The idea was that a sinner, one who lives for himself, will end up having his wealth distributed to others involuntarily—even to those he does not like—while "a good person," one who lives with others in mind, will consciously leave an inheritance for future generations. The question for us is how "good" parents will distribute this inheritance so that it will be a blessing and not a curse to our descendants.

Most of us have seen the devastation of young adults who have received enormous financial inheritances that they were unprepared to handle. Such financial legacies can remove a young person's motivation for productivity and lessen her potential contribution to society. German poet Johann Wolfgang von Goethe has been quoted with saying, "What from your father's heritage is lent, earn it anew to really possess it." Unfortunately, many young adults who receive large financial sums fail to "really possess it." They hold it in small regard or use it as they please.

So, how do parents responsibly leave a financial inheritance to their children and their grandchildren? If the inheritance is relatively small, the task can be fairly straightforward, although it is still essential to have a will and designate who is to receive what. When the value of an estate increases, the process of disbursing the legacy becomes more complicated, and in the affluence of Western culture, many parents have accumulated thousands or even more in assets. However, no matter the size of the inheritance, it is important to plan well. Passing your material legacy on in a responsible manner is a concern for many, especially if, for whatever reason, you intend that your assets are disbursed fairly but not necessarily identically among your children or others. Remember, too, that a material legacy will also address your wishes about charity and other such matters, including allowance for caregiving.

Rob and Joyce's Story

Rob and Joyce Morgan had been married for forty-four years and had three children and five grandchildren; two of their children were married and one was single. They lived in the large house where they had raised their children. Some years after retirement, they decided to scale down, get a smaller house, and dispose of some furnishings. They discussed their decision with the children and asked if any of them wanted to buy the house. Since none of them did, they sold the house and found a new one. They selected the furnishings they wanted to keep.

To leave any size estate without a will is to allow the state to dictate how the estate will be distributed.

Then Rob and Joyce invited the three children to the house to choose what they wanted of the remaining items. When the selections were all made, Rob and Joyce were pleased that none of their children had disagreed with the choices of the others and that everyone was happy with what they had received. Such a plan helped avoid resentment and misunderstanding among the children. Proper arrangements will be fair, equitable, and thoughtful, modeling positive negotiation and maintaining healthy relationships among family members.

Once Rob and Joyce had moved to their new home, they began to assess their monetary estate. Since two of their children were raising their families and needed the money more now than they would later, they checked with their financial planner and learned what the tax laws in their state allowed them to give to each child as nontaxable income. They also sought counsel about how to disburse their funds—both now and after their deaths—among their married children and their single one. Would an equal three-way split be best? Or more for the families with children? Would the family with three children inherit more than the one with two?

The Morgans demonstrated several important aspects of passing on a financial legacy. First, their actions underlined the importance of a will. To leave any size estate without a will is to allow the state to dictate how the estate will be distributed. They also knew the value of consulting an accountant or a financial planner as they made their decisions. These professionals should be aware of changing tax laws and often can save clients a great deal of money by their suggestions. They knew that some of the money could be given to children before the death of the parents. Giving your offspring part of the estate early is often a wise tax move and proves helpful to the family. They demonstrated that parents can help their children through various financial vehicles, and they involved their children in the distribution of personal assets.

In the Morgans' case, their children were all successful, earning viable incomes and enjoying a reasonable quality of life. But some families have grown children who are irresponsible or who have destructive lifestyles. Should they be treated identically to those living responsible lives? Answers to these questions are varied and require much planning and wisdom. Many families have particular situations for which they need to seek expert help; for instance, when parents have a child who is physically impaired and needs special care or an adult child who is mentally or emotionally unable to handle money. They must make financial plans that will provide the care that is needed but within wise guidelines.

Some adult siblings experience tension over who was the more present caregiver for the aging parent(s). In other families, there have been remarriages that resulted in children from a first marriage getting nothing when an estate has been left to a second spouse. These and other scenarios ideally should be addressed and refreshed as best as you can before you are not there to indicate your wishes. "This is not a one and done conversation. Family dynamics are constantly changing," said one expert.[2]

Whatever the size of your estate, it's important to make decisions instead of leaving these matters in the hands of your grown children after your death or even if you become incapacitated. An excellent resource is *Splitting Heirs: Giving Your Money and Things to Your Children Without Ruining Their Lives* by Ron Blue and Jeremy White.

MORE THAN MONEY

As was said, legacy is an inheritance handed down from one generation to the next, something by which our descendants remember us. In a legal sense, a legacy is a deposition of personal property that is made by terms of a will, "something transmitted by or received from an ancestor or predecessor."[3] But its impact is usually deeper than material—our legacy will have a powerful influence on the lives of those who follow us. As we saw in the stories of Art and Matt, the most important legacies are not monetary, but emotional, spiritual, and moral, and they center around the character of the person leaving them.

Legacies from the past affect a family's future. We all know families with longstanding reputations of good character—kindness, honesty, decency, upstanding behavior, and more. We all know fortunate people who inherited such a positive legacy from their parents and grandparents, and we can see the great advantages to them in terms of self-esteem and emotional well-being. On the other hand, we are aware of the handicaps borne by those who are plagued by a parent's negative legacy of character and behavior. While we like to believe that an individual can overcome any disadvantage, we all know that what has happened in our families can seem either a blessing or a curse on our lives.

A Legacy in Personal Lives

Doyne and Nancy have been married thirty-five years. They have four children and three grandchildren. Doyne came from a family with a poor legacy. His grandfather and father were hard men; the grandfather had grown up in an impoverished family, passing on stinginess and fear to his children. His father was unable to display affection for his wife and children and had a silent dread of never having enough. Doyne suffered in this household and decided to join the army immediately after high school.

His military experience was valuable, giving him the confidence he so lacked because of unspoken messages from his father. He now learned that he was competent and bright. After his tour ended, he entered college and did quite well. There he met Nancy, "the most beautiful woman I had ever seen," he recalls with delight. She had been reared in a happy, stable family. The couple dated and soon married, and from her experiences of growing up in a healthy household, Nancy became a loving and supportive spouse. Doyne loved her deeply and was profoundly appreciative of the sound parenting she had received. Nancy's mother and father had demonstrated to her what a family could and should be.

In Nancy's parents, Doyne found the family he had never had. They made time for outings with the couple, and her father showed

Doyne the trick to making homemade hashbrowns. His in-laws gave him the love and understanding he craved.

"When her father first gave me a hug," Doyne remembers, "I didn't know how to respond. I had never been hugged by a man before. When her mother said 'I love you,' I choked up."

Doyne's life took such a different turn when he met Nancy and then came to know her parents. Today the wonderful legacy of Nancy's parents is reaching beyond their own family to their grandchildren.

But there is more to Doyne's story. Because of the problems in his childhood home, the relationships among him and his siblings, Martha and Bob, had always been strained. The three tended to avoid each other because contact between them brought back the terrible feelings from childhood. As Doyne learned more of the values of a close and loving family, he tried to have more contact with Martha and Bob. At first this was difficult, especially for his sister and brother, but Doyne continued to keep in touch with them, and eventually they all spent a Christmas together.

"We talked about how lousy our Christmas holidays were as children. We talked and we cried. It was painful, but it was good. It was the first time we had ever talked about our heartache with each other."

Doyne is looking forward to the time when the three of them can experience real warmth and love for one another. He believes it will happen. His only regret is that no healing can take place with their parents, who died several years ago.

Doyne's story demonstrates how a family that experiences high self-esteem pulls together. Doyne received such affirming response from Nancy's parents that he was able to reach out to his two siblings, wanting to come together even though for years they had been apart. A family with high self-esteem enjoys being together and also keeping in touch when they are apart. The good feelings they have about each other provide a wonderful sense of stability and security in a pressured world. These positive feelings are determined primarily by the legacy of older family members, including those who have died.

LEGACIES FOR OUR CHILDREN'S CHARACTER

All the legacies we leave our children will affect their personal character. Three nonmaterial legacies greatly influence our children, so let's consider each: the moral, spiritual, and emotional legacies.

A Moral Legacy

Morality has to do with our belief of what is right and wrong. The moral legacy we leave our children—how well they internalize our standards of right and wrong—usually reflects how well we modeled our own moral code. We may never have put that code into writing, but we carry it around every day.

Our children discover our moral code by listening to us. When we say, "Don't ever steal," we are revealing that we believe stealing is wrong. When a father says, "Always help others when you can," he is stating his belief that it is right to help others when it is in one's power to do so. Parents make such statements throughout their kids' childhood, and children hear and mentally record them. They observe our lives and see how closely we live by our professed morality. The closer our behavior corresponds to our stated beliefs about right and wrong, the more respect our children have for us and the greater our moral legacy.

Arria acknowledged the moral legacy she had received when she said at her mother's funeral, "I know that my mother was not perfect, but she came as close as anyone I've ever known. She taught us what was right and wrong and, more importantly, she modeled it for us. On the occasions when she did wrong, she always admitted it and asked our forgiveness.

"I remember one time when I had begged her all afternoon to take me to the park. She was on her hands and knees mopping the floors and was extremely tired. When I asked her for the umpteenth time, 'Momma, please take me to the park,' she snapped. She hurled her wet rag across the room and yelled at me. Then she suddenly stopped and called me to her. She hugged me and said, 'Oh darling, I'm so sorry. I shouldn't have lost my temper like that. Please forgive me.' She kept me in her arms until I stopped crying. She promised, 'I'll take you to the park as soon as I'm done with this floor.' I'll never forget that. I learned she wasn't perfect, but I learned the power of her apology. I only hope that I'm as good a mother to my two children as she was to me."

When your children observe a positive pattern, they will often copy it.

On the other hand, Casey shared the negative moral legacy he had received from his mother. "I hate to say it, but my mother was all talk. She told us what was right and wrong, but she didn't live by her own teachings. She yelled and screamed at us, and often hit us even when we hadn't done anything wrong. If we irritated her in the least way, we could expect that she would lash out either physically or verbally. After my sister and I left home, she started running around on my dad. Eventually she left him and moved in with another man. For the next several years, it was from one man to another. She had always told us that adultery was wrong and that we should never live with someone unless we were married. My sister and I could not believe her behavior. She was doing everything she told us not to do. This went on until she got cancer and died six months later. Dad took care of her hospital bills, and we all went to see her regularly. Toward the end, she told us that she was sorry for what she had done. I guess we all forgave her. I know I tried, but it didn't take away the memory. I still have an empty, disappointed feeling when I think about her. I don't suppose it will ever go away."

Arria's and Casey's responses to their mothers' lives should make clear a guiding principle for improving the moral legacy we're preparing for our children: practice your moral standards. When your children observe a positive pattern, they will often copy it.

As with all legacies, a moral legacy becomes the property of your children when you die. It is theirs—to enjoy or endure. From this legacy, they receive encouragement or disappointment. Negative or positive, your children have no choice but to receive your legacy. What they do with it, of course, is their responsibility. Those children who have been given a positive moral legacy receive a valuable asset for future living. Conversely, those who are given a negative moral legacy receive a liability with which they must learn to cope.

> The great use of life is to spend it for something that will outlast it.
> — William James

205

A Spiritual Legacy

As morality has to do with what we believe to be right and wrong, so spirituality has to do with what we believe about the nonmaterial world. Even if you don't go to church or the synagogue, your spirituality is pervasive—it's part of who you are. It affects your moral and emotional responses, as well as your financial practices. And it will influence your children.

Kent went to church as a small child but doesn't remember much about it. There was big church time when he sat with his parents and everyone around him was taller than he was. Then he and the other children were taken to little church time, where there were stories and clay and goldfish crackers and juice, maybe clapping hands to songs. When his older brother joined Little League, the family went to see all his games, many of which were on Sunday mornings. After that, Kent doesn't think the family picked up the habit of going to church again. "The boys can decide what they believe when they grow up," Mom said. "Right," Dad agreed. "No use jamming our beliefs down their throats."

"My father said he was a Christian, but I never saw any evidence of it. If he was a Christian, then I don't want to be one."

When Kent met Krista and they started talking about marriage and a family, they never discussed religion. It hadn't been a part of either of their upbringings, and since they had both had happy childhoods and were close to their families, what was the point? Unfortunately, Kent and Krista's life together didn't turn out to be as idyllic as they expected. Between underemployment and career setbacks, miscarriages, the sudden death of Kent's father, and a basement that kept flooding, they were continually beaten down by the disappointments of life. They had not developed friendships with anyone who could encourage them to see greater purpose in life than what was before them. They had no anchor to lean on through difficulties and no sense that there was a God who cared.

Chad, on the other hand, received a strong religious legacy from his mother. When he was twenty-three his mother died, but Chad was confident. "One thing I know for sure," he said. "My mother is in heaven. My mother was a godly woman. When I was little, she read Bible stories to me every night and explained what it meant to be a Christian. She told me about the teachings of Jesus, about His death and resurrection, about God's love and forgiveness. But more importantly, she lived her Christian faith. I saw her practice her beliefs every day. Even in her sickness, her faith was strong. I know I will see her again in heaven."

In contrast, the spiritual legacy Spencer received was anything but positive. He has little interest in spiritual matters, mainly because of an inconsistent father. "My father said he was a Christian, but I never saw any evidence of it. I never saw him read the Bible and seldom heard him pray. He didn't go to church. He often cursed and when he lost his temper, he was anything but Christlike. My poor mother put up with more junk from him than any woman should have to endure.

> The greatest legacy one can pass on to one's children and grandchildren is not money or other material things accumulated in one's life, but rather a legacy of character and faith.
> — Billy Graham

If my father was a Christian, then I don't want to be one."

Parents will leave some sort of spiritual legacy, whether positive, negative, or indifferent.

In many families, the adult children have different value systems than the parents, and some of these parents feel that they have failed and give up hope. Yet, nothing is gained if they become down-hearted. Parents need to be beacons of hope, not only for children who have different values, but for the rest of the family. Christian parents who lose heart have forgotten that God is always with us, in good times and bad. He is always ready to help in every situation.

The spiritual needs of our children are great; and passing on a spiritual legacy gives them significance, purpose, and noble values that can benefit future generations.

Some parents have also forgotten that an adult child can change. Even when children have drifted away from the faith in which they were raised, loving parents will never give up, but will pray continually. Most important of all, caring parents will remember that their strongest influence on their children is their own example. By demonstrating faithfulness to God, parents are role models of lives well lived. The parents' consistent loyalty to God can be a powerful means of helping adult children return to the flock of the faithful.

To those readers who are Christians, remember that those who wander from the Christian faith often return when they have children of their own and realize that these little ones must develop a value system. As new parents, they conclude that the only value system worth having is one based on a deep religious faith and a trust in Jesus Christ. They return to a Christian value system based on grace and forgiveness. Though the adult children may have lost much during their spiritual wandering, becoming parents helps them realize what they almost fully lost.

It is critical for parents of adult children to hold on to their spiritual heritage, not only for themselves but also to give this legacy to their children and grandchildren. The spiritual needs of our children are great; and passing on a spiritual legacy gives them significance, purpose, and noble values that can benefit future generations.

> Someone is sitting in the shade today because someone planted a tree a long time ago.
> — Warren Buffett

An Emotional Legacy

The emotional legacy we leave depends largely on how we meet the emotional needs of our children. If those needs are met, they receive love, wholeness, and balance—a positive emotional legacy. But if they are not met, the children receive insecurity, low self-esteem, and often fear—a negative emotional legacy.

The most fundamental emotional need of children is the need to feel loved. Most parents sincerely love their children, but this does not guarantee that the children will *feel* loved. In chapter 1, you read about the five love languages and how each child feels he or she is loved when parents speak his specific love language and when they love without conditions, showing a "no matter what" kind of love. When your child's need for unconditional love is met, he will do better in school, have a more positive attitude, need less corrective discipline for misbehavior, and have a more stable emotional foundation that will serve him well throughout his lifetime.

Other significant emotional needs are the needs for security or safety, the need for self-worth or significance, the need to belong or be accepted, and the need for productivity or accomplishment. When these are met, children grow up to have a healthy emotional life and are able to cope with the stresses of adult life.

When these needs are not met, however, children grow up with many internal struggles that follow them for decades. As an adult, Allison lived with such struggles; she never was sure her mother loved her.

"I know now that Mom's family of origin had a lot to do with the way she treated me, but as a child, I couldn't understand that. I just felt she didn't love me."

"I've finally come to understand that my mother meant well," she said during one counseling session. "It took me a long time to realize this, but it has helped me cope with all the pain. I felt that Mom had no time for me. Her harsh, cutting words rang in my mind for years and her physical abuse left deep emotional scars. When she would punish me, she wouldn't speak to me or look at me for several days. When I'd ask if she loved me, she would reply, 'It doesn't do any good to discipline a kid and then turn around and love on them.'"

Allison continued. "I never heard my mother say she loved me. The only time she would touch me was when I was sick. I'd do anything to try to please her. I know now that Mom's family of origin had a lot to do with the way she treated me, but as a child, I couldn't understand that. I just felt she didn't love me. I always struggled with self-esteem and felt that I could never accomplish anything. No matter what I did, it was never good enough. I know now that this is not true, but it took a lot of counseling to find healing from the wounds of my childhood. I tried to help Mom when she was sick, and I hope she knew that I loved her. But even in her sickness, I could never really feel close to her. When she died, I went into a deep depression, because I knew that things could never be any different. I have found a measure of healing, but I still feel a great disappointment that I never felt close to my mother." Thousands of other adult children can identify with the kind of pain Allison has experienced.

ADDITIONAL THOUGHTS ON LEGACY

Memories

As parents of adult children, we will also leave a legacy of memories. In one sense, memories are all any of us possess of the past, and we should be doing our best to ensure that our children have positive memories that can sustain them in the years to come.

However, the memories of shared activities are not as vital as the feelings we had and have about those events. Our most important feelings are the ones we have in everyday life, for they exert a powerful influence on our long-term memory. Because of this, the way we parents conduct ourselves consistently is what really counts. It is crucial that we take care to treat family members with courtesy, respect, kindness, love, and gentleness. Also, we should avoid anger, criticism, harshness, and loudness as much as possible. Yes, we will all make mistakes, but if we are honest with ourselves, we can identify those mistakes and seek to avoid repeating the behaviors. Even if mistakes have been made in the past and the children are well grown, as has been said before, if you feel you should confess your shortcomings to your children and start a new path of making memories, take the initiative and do so.

The Long Haul

We have been talking about various legacies we leave those who follow us. A key part of our legacy we can leave is our personal character and integrity. This legacy has great impact on how we are remembered, by our children and in generations to follow.

There is nothing that hurts as much as a negative change in a parent's integrity and behavior. When a person rejects the values she has instilled in her children, it is a blow that will stun children to a degree from which they may never recover. The most common example today is a person who has been a good parent and spouse and then decides that he needs a change and divorces his spouse. This is so prevalent that many people regard it as normal behavior. Another growing phenomenon is older adults choosing to live together though unmarried.

Carol, a sixty-eight-year-old widow, brought great pain to her daughter when she decided to live with a sixty-six-year-old widower. "I'm not sure I love him," she said, "but I enjoy being with him, and it will save both of us a lot of money. If the young people can do it, why can't we?"

> Legacy is not what I did for myself. It's what I'm doing for the next generation.
> — Vitor Belfort

"Because you are my mother," her forty-five-year-old daughter said. "What kind of example do you think this sets for Jennifer and Traci? I can't believe you're doing this. Don't you have any concern for your own grandchildren?"

Carol's behavior contradicted how she had raised her daughter. In fact, Carol had often criticized younger couples who lived together without being married. Carol's legacy is in jeopardy. When Jennifer and Traci heard about their grandmother's behavior, they were very upset and confused. She is in danger of losing the respect of those she loves most.

It is not easy to maintain your character and integrity over many years. This is especially true when sacrifice is called for, and all of us meet situations where it is. Thank God for those who are able to take care of their responsibilities over a lifetime and who are willing to give up what they desire for the sake of those in their care. Giving oneself for the sake of others is increasingly rare.

Our society places little value on sacrificial living, on maintaining one's principles, on telling the truth, or on keeping promises. In such an environment, it takes real strength of character and all the support we can find to live righteously. Yet, though society may not praise people of sound character, their children and grandchildren dearly love and appreciate them.

Character and Stability

We talk of character and integrity, and yet perhaps we need to define them. We want our children to have these qualities, but just what does this mean? Character is the totality of who we genuinely are inside. It is all that we think and feel, what we truthfully stand for, which is expressed in our pattern of behavior.

Integrity is a part of our character and is best known by three behaviors: telling the truth, keeping one's promises, and taking responsibility for one's behavior.

All of us have fallen short at times, but we should not give up. Again, if we need to make restitution, we can do so. We can ask forgiveness and make necessary amends.

A by-product of good character is a legacy of stability, when a parent has made good decisions and exhibited clear thinking over many years. Children watch when parents go through tough times, and they learn how to handle difficult situations from what they see. Where the parents have given this legacy of stability, the adult children will ask in their own troubled times, "What would Mom and Dad do? How would they think this through? What advice would they seek from others? How long would they allow themselves to decide what to do? How would they pray about it? How would they know when the decision had to be made?"

THE POWER OF PRAYER

Let's close this chapter with one other powerful vehicle for influencing adult children: prayer. In recent years, social researchers have begun to take seriously the influence of prayer. Numerous studies have shown that the healing process in persons treated by physicians is more effective if the treatment is accompanied by prayer.[4] These researchers are discovering what sincere religious people have always known—prayer changes things and people.

For those in the Judeo-Christian tradition, prayer assumes the existence of a personal and infinite God who cares deeply about His creatures and who has invited them to reciprocate His love. Jews know the love of being called God's chosen people;[5] Christians believe that love is demonstrated by God sending His only Son, Jesus of Nazareth, as a sacrifice for people's transgressions.[6] It is this reciprocating love relationship that many have found to be the most satisfying of all relationships and that profoundly affects family dynamics.

The heart of your legacy to your children is not material but spiritual. Praying for your children daily—and it's just as important or more so if they're grown—is a living legacy that can influence their behavior now and for years to come. The praying parent not only becomes a wiser person but is forever an influential parent.

———

As you give these legacies—moral, spiritual, emotional, material, memories, and character for the long haul—be grateful that you have the opportunity of watching your children enter adulthood and continue the legacy you have begun. Remember that they are on their own, yet you can continue to influence them for good. Through your character and integrity, you may influence them to adopt your pattern. Through your prayer, you can find both peace for yourself and influence upon your children's spiritual lives. Parenting your adult child at times may be challenging, even difficult, but it is a blessing too, as you influence the next generation and generations to come.

eleven

What Can
I Do When . . .

In this short chapter, we'll address some other common issues when relating to your adult child.

What can I do when my adult child is grieving?

Tragedy is a reality. Your adult child may experience the break-up of a dating relationship, or the death of a spouse or child, or the loss of a job, or the death of a close friend, or some other tragedy. Grief is the deep sorrow that one feels when they have experienced a personal tragedy.

Grief may express itself with tears, difficulty sleeping, headaches, fatigue, a sense of heaviness, or other physical signs of stress. Sadness, anger, confusion, frustration are common emotions when one is experiencing grief. The journey through grief is not a predictable pattern. Each individual must walk their own path. We do know that grief does not go away quickly but may linger for a year or more. Even years later, one may still experience seasons of grief as he or she reflects on their loss.

As the parent of an adult child who is experiencing grief, you may be allowed the privilege of walking with them. This is usually true when you have a close relationship with your adult child. If you have this opportunity, here are some guidelines.

- Engage them in conversations about their loss. Grief is processed by sharing.
- If you live geographically close, invite them to dinner.
- If you live at a distance, call, or have video chat meetings with them regularly.
- Let them know that you are open for them to contact you anytime, day or night.
- Don't try to rush them into "getting over" their grief.
- Be empathetic with their emotions. "I can only imagine how painful it is."
- Share memories you have of their loved one, if death is the reason for their grief.
- If loss of a job is the source of their grief, use your influence to explore job possibilities.
- Take initiative to discover local Grief Share or similar groups that may be available.
- Pray for your adult child, but don't preach to them.

If you are estranged from your adult child, their grief may open the door to the possibility of reconciliation. Reach out and let them know that you love them. Apologize for your past failures, and invite them to meet with you. If they are open, invite them to join you in seeing a counselor. You cannot force your estranged child to let you back into their lives, but you can open the door.

What can I do when one adult child is outshone by her siblings?

Andy and Mary's oldest child, Priscilla, is a certified public accountant. Next comes Logan, a high school principal. Glenna is the baby in the family and is a sophomore in college but has no idea what she wants her major to be.

She knows she does not want to be a CPA or an educator. She does not feel smart enough to do either of those. She has taken all the general requirements in college but is thinking of dropping out because she does not know what she wants to do. She has never felt as smart as her siblings. What she really enjoys is dancing, but she does not think she is good enough to dance professionally. She knows that her parents love her, but she feels they are not very proud of her.

Glenna's parents strongly want her to find something she enjoys doing, but they also want her to be able to obtain a job to support herself. If I were talking to her parents, here is what I would advise. Have a conference with Mom, Dad, and Glenna to discuss her future. Tell Glenna that they love her very much and want to do anything they can to help her discover her dreams. Ask Glenna to tell them how she feels about where she is in life. Whatever she says, listen with empathy; put themselves in her shoes and try to see the world through her eyes. If she says, "Everyone in the family is so smart, I just don't feel that I fit in," express understanding: "I can see how you could feel that way. That is not how we view you, but we can see that is how you feel. What do you think we could do to help you find your dream for your life?" If she has no dream, suggest that she get an appointment with the school counselor who tests students for their aptitude and what vocations are possibilities for them. In doing this, she might find a dream.

If she does not take action, then explore what is available at her college or another organization in town and give her the contact information. Ultimately, if she does not call for an appointment, you might make an appointment for her. It is likely that in this setting, she will find a field of interest she has never considered. If she is unwilling and has signs of depression, then individual counseling may be necessary.

As parents we cannot make our adult children do anything. However, we can seek to help them take steps that they would not take on their own initiative. Communicate the reality that each individual is unique. We are not all meant to be educators and accountants, but we all have an important role to play in life. As parents we want to help our children find and follow their dream. We do not help them by criticizing their behavior, but by communicating that we believe in them and know that they will find their place in the world.

What can I do when I don't think my adult child's career choice is appropriate/ good enough/ worthy of his/her abilities?

Most parents want to see their child reach their potential for God and good in the world. However, sometimes our ideas of what that looks like are different from that of our adult child. It may also be different from God's plans for that individual. Sometimes we push our vocational ideas on our children without regard to their own ideas.

A young man who had just finished four years of medical school said to me: "I never wanted to be a doctor. I still don't want to be a doctor. My father pushed me to go to medical school against my wishes. I agreed, but I am more convinced than ever that this is not for me. So I'm not going to take a medical residency. I don't want to hurt my father, but I cannot let him live his dreams through my life." He decided to pursue a far different vocation.

As parents, we must be careful not to do what this father did. In our culture we have exalted certain vocations above others. We have failed to recognize that any vocation that involves helping people is a worthy vocation. We must also remember that each of us is unique. We have different interests, abilities, and desires. We must give our adult children the freedom to choose their own vocation. We are free to express our thoughts and opinions but recognize that they must live their own lives.

What can I do when I have nothing to talk about with my adult child?

When this happens, it normally reveals that we have allowed an emotional distance to develop between the parent and adult child. There are many reasons for this. Sometimes the parent has become so involved in living their own lives that they have failed to build an emotional connection with their child through the years.

I remember standing at the graveside of a father, when I asked his son: "What kind of relationship did you have with your father?" His response surprised me. He said, "I never really got to know my father." When I asked, "Why?" he told me that his father's work schedule kept him away from home most weeks. On Saturdays, he played golf with his friends, and on Sunday, he slept till noon and then watched football on television. "I just never spent much time with him." I walked away deeply saddened. So, when you have nothing to talk about with your adult child, the first question might be, what has been my role in creating this situation? What you discover may call for an apology, which can be the first step in building a bridge between the two of you.

On the other hand, the problem may lie with your adult child. There are many young adult men and women who became so obsessed with technology, sports, dancing, and so on that this obsession followed them into adulthood. They literally spend all of their free time with what they're so crazy about, making no effort to enter into the world of their parents. So emotional distance has become a lifestyle. One step for parents in this situation might be to express interest in the thing with which their adult child is so enamored. It may not be your natural desire, but it can be the street that helps you enter their world. It begins by asking questions about their interests and then learning to talk about things that interest them. Reading books or articles in the field of their interests will give you fodder for conversation.

What can I do when I just don't feel close to their spouse?

There may be numerous reasons for this disconnect. Some parents, for different reasons, did not like the person their child was dating and voiced disapproval. Now the adult child has married the person, and you are still not happy about it. If this is the case, it is time for you to adapt to reality. Accept that your adult child made a choice and out of respect for your child, choose to seek to build a relationship with their spouse. As you get to know them, you may find you develop a close relationship. The process may involve having lunches, shopping, taking walks, or any number of activities with their spouse. Friendships are built by spending time together.

Another common reason that you may not feel close to their spouse is personality differences. Personality is our patterned way of thinking, behaving, and feeling. Maybe they are the kind of person who sees the glass half empty rather than half full, and their negative perspective irritates you. Or perhaps they are not organized, and that bothers you.

There are strengths and weaknesses in all of our personalities. Certain personality traits may push us away and other personality traits draw us to that person. So, the parent might ask the question: "What is there about him or her that irritates me?" Your answer may well identify the particular trait that stands in the way of a close relationship. Any one of us can work on aspects of our personality when we recognize that it is not helping our relationships; however, as your child's parent, you are not likely the best person to point out the weaknesses of their spouse. The answer is far more likely to come in your choosing to accept that aspect of who they are and not allowing it to keep you from spending time with and seeking to develop a close relationship.

What can I do when I have a new relationship in my own life?

Divorce or the death of a spouse often leaves a parent single again. In due time, they may begin to develop a relationship with someone else, which may progress to dating and sometimes lead to marriage. Adult children do not always agree with your decision to get involved with this new person. In fact, sometimes they strongly criticize your behavior. They may express their displeasure with angry words and may even withdraw from you. So, what is a parent to do?

My first suggestion is to seek to see things through the eyes of your adult children. Perhaps they had a strong emotional bond with their biological parent, who is now gone. This is often true in the case of the death of your former spouse. They have a hard time seeing you get intimate with someone else. You are creating a whole new world for them. When you look at the world through their eyes, you can affirm their feelings if not their behavior. With such affirmation, you often open the door for civil dialogue in which you can share your perspective. If you express understanding of their thoughts and feelings, they may come to do the same for your thoughts and feelings.

As a parent, ultimately you must make the decision you feel is best. Prayer for God's guidance would be extremely important. If your decision is to pursue this new relationship and perhaps to marry the person, in due time, your adult children will likely begin to warm up to the new reality. If not, then you must learn to live with a fractured relationship with your adult child. We cannot make our children accept our decisions, just as our adult child cannot make you accept some of their decisions with which you disagree. However, the loving response in both situations is to keep the door open, seek to engage in open communication, and always express your love for each other.

What can I do when I feel like I have no option but to break off the relationship with my adult child?

There are two situations when this may be the best, though not the desired, decision. First is the physical, emotional, and mental health of the parent. Sometimes the parent has done everything they can to help their adult child live a responsible life, all to no avail. The adult child continues to follow life-destroying practices in spite of all the parents have done. Such behavior can ultimately negatively impact the parent's physical, emotional, and mental health, bringing the parent to the breaking point. To continue the pattern they have followed will lead to the detriment of their own lives. They will then find themselves unable to do anything. When signs of such deterioration begin to appear, it is time to break off the relationship while you still have the ability to do so.

The second situation when such a break-off should be considered is when the parent's behavior is enabling the adult child to continue in a self-destructive lifestyle. Their physical and financial help is no longer helping, but rather encouraging an ill-chosen pathway. The attitude of the parent is: "We love you too much to continue to enable a lifestyle that is destroying you. Our love for you will not allow us to continue this pattern." Such a decision is emotionally difficult, but it is the most loving thing you can do.

Some adult children will not change their destructive lifestyle until they end up in the pigpen. Perhaps you remember the story of the prodigal son recorded in the Bible. He talked his father into giving him his inheritance while the parents were still alive. The father chose to do so. The son left and wasted his inheritance in pleasure, seeking sinful behavior. When the money was all gone, he ended up working for a farmer by feeding pigs. He even found himself eating the pigs' slop.

When he hit bottom, he remembered that the hired men who worked for his father were much better off than he was with the pigs. So, he decided to go home and say to his father: "I have sinned against heaven and against you. I am no longer worthy to be called your son; make me like one of your hired men."[1] So, he returned home. His father welcomed him with open arms and treated him lovingly. I have always found it interesting that his father did not leave the farm and go seeking him. He waited until his son's lifestyle caught up with him, and he willingly returned home. He kept the farm going so that when his son decided to come home, there was a home still available.

So, when we release our wayward adult children to God, we focus on staying physically, emotionally, and mentally healthy. We keep our marriage moving in a positive direction, and we continue in our vocation of serving others in the name of Christ. When our wayward son or daughter chooses to come home, they will be met with open arms.

Acknowledgments

It was my privilege to work closely with Dr. Ross Campbell when we first wrote a book on parenting your adult child. I grew to greatly respect his years of research and clinical practice as a psychiatrist. His devotion to Christ knit our hearts together. I am deeply grateful to him for his part in writing this book. I anticipate our reunion in heaven.

I also want to express my deep gratitude for Pam Pugh and her excellent work in updating this edited version you hold in your hand. She invested many hours in this project, and I genuinely appreciate her excellent work. I also want to thank Brandi Davis for her work on the interior design and typesetting for this new version, as well as Kaylee Dunn for designing the new cover.

Notes

CHAPTER 1. YOUR RELATIONSHIP WITH YOUR ADULT CHILD

1. Jerry Scott and Jim Borgman, "Zits," January 4, 2024.
2. If you still have children or teens in your home, or are even raising grandchildren, I recommend *How to Really Love Your Child* and *How to Really Love Your Teen*, both by Ross Campbell. The chapters on discipline are especially helpful.
3. The full proverb, "Start children off on the way they should go, and even when they are old they will not turn from it" (Proverbs 22:6), was written by Solomon.
4. The love languages—how to learn them and how to use them—are discussed in more detail in the book *The 5 Love Languages* and other books in the series. You may also visit 5lovelanguages.com.
5. Psalm 127:3 and Psalm 103:17.

CHAPTER 2. WHEN YOUR ADULT CHILD IS STUCK

1. "Coping with Parent Guilt," COPE, https://www.cope.org.au/new-parents/emotional-health-new-parents/parent-guilt/.
2. God often is described as a father, and the Scriptures indicate He has the compassionate heart of a loving father. See Psalm 103:13–15; Luke 15:20–24; 2 Corinthians 1:3–4.
3. Jim Spiewak, "US Surgeon General Report Sounds Alarm: We're More Connected but Lonelier than Ever," July 18, 2023, https://kutv.com/

news/utahs-state-of-mind/us-surgeon-general-report-sounds-alarm-were-more-connected-but-lonelier-than-ever-licensed-clinical-therapist-jenn-oxborrow-social-media-platforms-our-epidemic-of-loneliness-and-isolation.

4. Proverbs 18:21.

CHAPTER 3. WHEN THE NEST ISN'T EMPTYING

1. Jill Savage, *Empty Nest, Full Life: Discovering God's Best for Your Next* (Chicago: Moody, 2019), 14.

2. Elizabeth Napolitano, "More Young Adults Are Living at Home Across the US. Here's Why," CBS News, September 21, 2023, https://www.cbsnews.com/news/gen-z-millennials-living-at-home-harris-poll/.

3. Savage, *Empty Nest, Full Life*, 13.

4. Gary Chapman, *Anger: Taming a Powerful Emotion* (Chicago: Moody, 2015), 31–32.

5. "4 Signs of Anger Problems," Discovery MD, May 10, 2021, https://discoverymd.com/4-signs-of-anger-problems/.

6. J. K. Ramsey, *The Lord Is My Courage* (Grand Rapids, MI: Zondervan Reflective, 2022), 27.

CHAPTER 4. WHEN YOUR CHILD MOVES BACK HOME

1. Jill Savage, *Empty Nest, Full Life: Discovering God's Best for Your Next* (Chicago: Moody, 2019), 54.

2. Elizabeth Napolitano, CBS News, September 21, 2023, "More Young Adults Are Living at Home Across the U. S. Here's Why," https://www.cbsnews.com/news/gen-z-millennials-living-at-home-harris-poll/.

CHAPTER 5. WHEN WELL-MEANING ISN'T ENOUGH

1. Kathleen Davis, "What Is Smiling Depression?," *Medical News Today*, April 22, 2020, https://www.medicalnewstoday.com/articles/smiling-depression.

2. Amy Morin, "Smiling Depression: When Things Aren't Quite What They Seem," Verywell Mind, November 14, 2023, https://www.verywellmind.com/what-is-smiling-depression-4775918.

3. Dan Witters, "US Depression Rates Reach New Highs," Gallup, May 17, 2023, https://news.gallup.com/poll/505745/depression-rates-reach-new-highs.aspx.

4. A resource that has helped many people understand and manage anger is *Anger: Taking a Powerful Emotion* by Gary Chapman.

5. Daniel K. Hall-Flavin, "What Is Passive-Aggressive Behavior? What Are Some of the Signs?," Mayo Clinic, https://www.mayoclinic.org/healthy-lifestyle/adult-health/expert-answers/passive-aggressive-behavior/faq-20057901.

6. Ibid.

7. "According to a study published by the National Library of Medicine, the drug's potency has tripled" in only a few years: in "Weed Is Stronger Now than Ever Before," Addiction Center, February 15, 2024, https://www.addictioncenter.com/drugs/marijuana/weed-stronger-than-before/.

8. "Pot Use Increasingly Linked to Addiction, Psychosis," *HealthDay News* in the *Chicago Tribune*, January 10, 2024, https://digitaledition.chicagotribune.com/infinity/article_share.aspx?guid=356ba533-5db8-4f27-aa42-e4e998e29f53.

9. Ibid.

10. "Words Matter: Preferred Language for Talking About Addiction," National Institute on Drug Abuse, https://nida.nih.gov/research-topics/addiction-science/words-matter-preferred-language-talking-about-addiction.

11. Lindsay Modglin, "Alcohol Statistics 2023," updated January 24, 2024, https://www.singlecare.com/blog/news/alcohol-statistics/.

12. "Deaths from Excessive Alcohol Use in the United States," Centers for Disease Control and Prevention, https://www.cdc.gov/alcohol/features/excessive-alcohol-deaths.html.

13. United States Department of Transportation, https://www.nhtsa.gov/risky-driving/drunk-driving.

14. "Legal Marijuana Is Making Roads Deadlier," Bloomberg Opinion Editorial Board, April 4, 2024, https://www.bloomberg.com/opinion/articles/2024-04-04/marijuana-legalization-has-made-us-roads-more-lethal.

15. Nickolaus Hayes, "Dry January Allows Us to Reboot Our Lives," *Chicago Tribune*, January 13, 2024, http://digitaledition.chicago tribune.com/infinity/article_share.aspx?guid=480b2fe4-2a1c-4274-9fa5-d112021f17d7.

16. Jennifer Wirth, "ADHD Statistics and Facts in 2023," Forbes, updated August 24, 2023, https://www.forbes.com/health/mind/adhd-statistics/.

17. "Symptoms: Attention Deficit Hyperactivity Disorder (ADHD)," NHS, https://www.nhs.uk/conditions/attention-deficit-hyperactivity-disorder-adhd/symptoms/.

18. "Adult Attention-Deficit/Hyperactivity Disorder (ADHD)," Mayo Clinic, https://www.mayoclinic.org/diseases-conditions/adult-adhd/diagnosis-treatment/drc-20350883.

CHAPTER 6. CARING FOR YOURSELF

1. Lynn Johnston, "For Better or for Worse," January 2, 2024, www.fborfw.com. Quoted with permission.

2. Matthew 20:28.

3. For example, Matthew 14:23, Mark 6:46–47, Luke 5:16, Luke 6:12.

4. Alcoholics Anonymous, The Twelve Steps, https://www.aa.org/the-twelve-steps.

5. "About Us," Celebrate Recovery, https://www.celebraterecovery.com/about.

CHAPTER 7. LIFESTYLE ISSUES

1. Scott M. Stanley and Galena K. Rhoades, "What's the Plan? Cohabitation, Engagement, and Divorce," Institute for Family Studies, April 2023, https://ifstudies.org/ifs-admin/resources/reports/cohabitation reportapr2023-final.pdf. Citing Barna Group, "Majority of Americans Now Believe in Cohabitation," Barna, June 14, 2016.

2. Ibid. Emphasis in source.

3. Emma Atkinson, "New DU Study Highlights Rises of Living Together Before Engagement," April 26, 2023, https://liberalarts.du.edu/news-events/all-articles/new-du-study-highlights-risks-living-together-engagement.

4. Ibid.

5. *The Ring Makes All the Difference* by Glenn T. Stanton is an excellent resource.
6. The Bible invites men and women who need wisdom to pray for it, and promises peace when we do pray. See for example James 1:5 and Philippians 4:6–7.
7. Samantha Schmidt, "Americans' View Flipped on Gay Rights. How Did Minds Change So Quickly?," *The Washington Post*, June 7, 2019, https://www.washingtonpost.com/local/social-issues/americans-views-flipped-on-gay-rights-how-did-minds-change-so-quickly/2019/06/07/ae256016-8720-11e9-98c1-e945ae5db8fb_story.html.
8. Ibid.
9. L. Eugene Burrus, "Christian Suffering and the Same-Sex Attracted," in *Marriage: Its Foundation, Theology, and Mission in a Changing World* (Chicago: Moody, 2018), 345.
10. Romans 3:23.
11. John 8:7.
12. Romans 8:1; 1 Peter 2:24.
13. Jill Savage, *Empty Nest, Full Life: Discovering God's Best for Your Next* (Chicago: Moody, 2019), 68–69.
14. Savage, *Empty Nest, Full Life*, 69.
15. Joe Dallas, "When Homosexuality Hits the Holidays: 5 Things to Remember When a Gay Loved One Joins the Family Gathering," https://restoryministries.org/2019/11/20/when-homosexuality-hits-the-holidays/.
16. Ibid.
17. Amy Morin, "What Is Dysphoria?," Verywell Mind, November 15, 2023, https://www.verywellmind.com/what-is-dysphoria-4588634.
18. David Ludden, "What Is Rapid Onset Gender Dysphoria?," *Psychology Today*, May 4, 2023, https://www.psychologytoday.com/us/blog/talking-apes/202304/what-is-rapid-onset-gender-dysphoria.
19. "Biblical View on Transgender Identity: A Primer for Parents and Strugglers," Focus on the Family, https://www.focusonthefamily.com/parenting/a-biblical-perspective-on-transgender-identity-a-primer-for-parents-and-strugglers/.
20. "Currently, about three-in-ten U. S. Adults (29%) are religious 'nones'—people who describe themselves as atheists, agnostics

or 'nothing in particular' when asked about their religious identity." Gregory A. Smith, "About Three-in-Ten US Adults Are Now Religiously Unaffiliated," Pew Research Center, December 21 2021, https://www.pewresearch.org/religion/2021/12/14/about-three-in-ten-u-s-adults-are-now-religiously-unaffiliated/.

21. Claire Nelson et al., "How Can Older Believers Better Support Gen Z?," *Christianity Today*, November 28, 2023, https://www.christianity today.com/ct/2023/november-web-only/how-can-older-believers-better-support-gen-z.html.

22. Ibid.

23. "10 Ways to Help When Adult Children Are Questioning Their Faith," Empty Nest Blessed, February 16, 2022, https://emptynest blessed.com/2022/02/16/when-adult-children-are-questioning-their-faith/.

24. Catherine Segars, "What to Do If Your Child Has Walked Away from the Faith," Crosswalk.com, November 2, 2022, https://www .crosswalk.com/family/parenting/what-to-do-if-your-child-has-walked-away-from-the-faith.html.

25. "Video Games Remain America's Favorite Pastime with More than 212 Million Americans Playing Regularly," Entertainment Software Association, July 20, 2023, https://www.theesa.com/news/video-games-remain-americas-favorite-pastime-with-more-than-212-million-americans-playing-regularly/.

26. "Gamer," Wikipedia, https://en.wikipedia.org/wiki/Gamer.

27. "How Can Video Games Impact Divorce?," Goldberg Jones, July 12, 2022, https://www.goldbergjones-sandiego.com/divorce/video-games-impact-divorce.

28. "49 Video Game Addiction Statistics: Most Addictive Games," MPower, January 18, 2023, https://mpowerwellness.com/video-game-addiction-statistics/.

29. Adapted from "Video Game Addiction Test for Parents," Game Quitters, https://gamequitters.com/video-game-addiction-test-for-parents/ and from Jeri Rochman, "Is My Adult Child Addicted to Video Games?," Advance LA, https://www.advancela.org/is-my-adult-child-addicted-to-video-games/. Both of these sites have helpful information.

30. "Are Video Games, Screens, Another Addiction?," Speaking of Health, July 1, 2022, https://www.mayoclinichealthsystem.org/hometown-health/speaking-of-health/are-video-games-and-screens-another-addiction.

31. ©2024 Amy Dickinson, "Ask Amy," January 1, 2024, *Chicago Tribune*. Distributed by Tribune Content Agency, LLC.

32. Veronica Dagher and Ashley Ebeling, "Asking Parents for Money," *Wall Street Journal*, December 28, 2023, https://wallstreetjournal-ny-app.newsmemory.com/?publink=0d0fe6c98_134ae60.

CHAPTER 8. BECOMING AN IN-LAW AND A GRANDPARENT

1. Taylor Orth and Carl Bailik, "Across Generations: Americans Describe Close Relationships with Their Grandparents and Grandchildren," YouGov, September 15, 2023, https://today.yougov.com/society/articles/46067-american-grandparent-grandchild-relationships.

2. Ibid.

3. Michael Sasso, "Older Americans Now Earn as Much as Younger Workers: Seniors in Labor Market Expected to Increase, Reshaping Workforce," Bloomberg News, in the *Chicago Tribune*, December 19, 2023, http://digitaledition.chicagotribune.com/infinity/article_share.aspx?guid=c9a299ba-00f7-424c-b383-8056a5671291.

4. Helen Dennis, "6 Factors That Influence How Grandparents Stay Connected with Grandchildren," Los Angeles Daily News, April 9, 2023, https://www.dailynews.com/2023/04/09/6-factors-that-influence-how-grandparents-stay-connected-with-grandchildren/.

5. Proverbs 17:6.

6. Gary Chapman and Ross Campbell, *The 5 Love Languages of Children: The Secret to Loving Children Effectively* (Chicago: Northfield Publishing, 2016).

7. A. J. Baime, "When Grandparents Are Called to Parent — Again," AARP, March 2, 2023, https://www.aarp.org/home-family/friends-family/info-2023/grandparents-become-parents-again.html.

8. Ibid. This article indicates that opioids are responsible for an increase in addiction and quotes Senator Susan Collins of Maine as saying, "I first got interested in this issue when I started seeing so many grandparents in Maine who were raising very young children.

In almost every case, the parent of the child had a crisis with drug addition or had been incarcerated."

9. Darcel Rockett, "Book Tells of Skipped Generation Households," *Chicago Tribune*, January 15, 2024, http://digitaledition.chicagotribune .com/infinity/article_share.aspx?guid=b35eca0d-643f-46f2-8618-ab2ccacd3bd6.

10. Teresa Kindred, "Nana's House," *Grandkids Matter*, September 16, 2020, https://grandkidsmatter.org/nanas-house/raising-your-grandkids-stories-wisdom-from-grandmothers/.

11. "Grandparents Raising Grandchildren," https://www.aamft.org/ Consumer_Updates/grandparents.aspx.

CHAPTER 9. MENDING RELATIONSHIPS AND RECONCILIATION

1. An excellent resource is *Hush: Moving from Silence to Healing after Childhood Sexual Abuse* by Nicole Braddock Bromley.

2. Exodus 34:6; Psalm 75:2; 1 Peter 2:24; 1 Peter 5:7.

3. The apostle John wrote that if we confess to God our sins, He "will forgive us our sins and purify us from all unrighteousness" (1 John 1:9). It is at this point that the parent is then able to accept forgiveness from God and from the adult child.

4. Matthew 6:12. In Ephesians 4:32, Christians are told to forgive "each other, just as in Christ God forgave you."

CHAPTER 10. YOUR LEGACY

1. Proverbs 13:22.

2. Ashlea Eberling, "How to Avoid Splitting Heirs," *Wall Street Journal*, April 9, 2024, citing Lena Haas, head of wealth management advice and solutions at Edward Jones, https://wallstreetjournal-ny-app .newsmemory.com/?publink=05ad17187_134d23d.

3. *Merriam-Webster*, s.v. "legacy (*n.*)," https://www.merriam-webster .com/dictionary/legacy.

4. This short article by Hayden Chin Mun Yee lists some of these studies: "The Influence of Prayer on Patient Recovery: A Scientific Review," Docquity, February 28, 2023, https://docquity.com/articles/ the-influence-of-prayer-on-patient-recovery-a-scientific-review/.

5. See Romans 5:8 and 1 John 4:19.

6. Known as the children of Israel in the Bible, Jews are called both the "chosen" people (see Deuteronomy 7:6–8) and the "apple of his eye" (Deuteronomy 32:9–10), an expression of closeness and care.

CHAPTER 11. WHAT CAN I DO WHEN . . .

1. You can read this story in Luke 15:11–32.

Simple ways to strengthen relationships.

TAKE THE LOVE LANGUAGE® QUIZ

DOWNLOAD FREE RESOURCES AND STUDY GUIDES

BROWSE THE LOVE LANGUAGE® GIFT GUIDE

SUBSCRIBE TO PODCASTS

SHOP THE STORE

SIGN UP FOR THE NEWSLETTER

Visit www.5lovelanguages.com

"I SAID I WAS SORRY! WHAT MORE DO YOU WANT?"

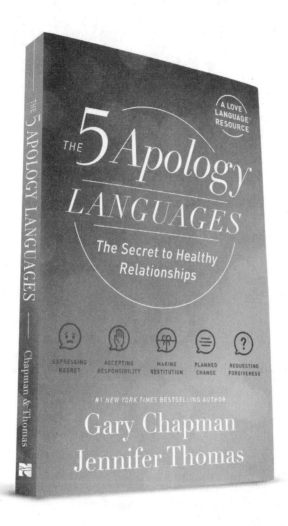